The
FRIENDSHIP
BOOK
of
Francis Gay

D. C. THOMSON & CO., LTD.
London Glasgow Manchester Dundee

A Thought
For Each Day
In 1987

The only way to have a friend is to be one
RALPH WALDO EMERSON

GOOD COMPANY

The paths of life may twist and bend.
Follow them gladly; walk with a friend.

JANUARY

THURSDAY—JANUARY 1.

IN her book " The Wind Blows ", Rita F. Snowdon quotes a verse I would like to pass on to you. I think it will give us all a good start as we set out on this New Year:

> *May every day of this New Year*
> *From January to December,*
> *Bring you, as you journey on,*
> *Something lovely to remember.*

A very happy New Year to you!

FRIDAY—JANUARY 2.

ONE of the features which attracts thousands of visitors to the Hunterian Art Gallery in Glasgow is a complete reconstruction of the house which belonged to Charles Rennie Mackintosh, the great Scottish architect, artist and furniture designer.

Its white walls, spacious rooms and austerely beautiful furniture in Mackintosh's unique style often bring gasps of admiration from those who see them. But the admiration is modified by some of the remarks made by those who pass through the rooms: "It's lovely, but I couldn't live in it"; "this looks the kind of room where nothing is ever out of place "; "it's beautiful — but somehow cold and unfriendly."

In other words, not a bit like our own homes, which may sometimes look untidy, but possess a warmth, a cosiness, a friendliness which has nothing to do with design or good taste, but everything to do with love.

THE FRIENDSHIP BOOK

COMPANIONSHIP is one of life's greatest treasures. To be able to share experiences, joys and sorrows with someone who understands and sympathises is surely beyond price. Yet it would be too much to expect a friendship never to have a rocky phase. At times we do get slightly out of step with each other. The French writer, Camus, has given this recipe for getting along together:

"Don't walk in front of me — I may not follow.

Don't walk behind me — I may not lead.

Just walk beside me — and be my friend."

A FAITHFUL friend is the medicine of life; and they that fear the Lord shall find him.

Ecclesiasticus 6, 16

THE Lady of the House loves a talk with old Willie Grant. He has a fund of stories and is never at a loss for a word — even if it is one he sometimes makes up as he goes along.

She came home delighted the other afternoon. Willie had been describing a row between two men over whose fault it was that a game of cards had been lost.

"There they were," said Willie, "the two of them glaring at one another. Isn't it daft to come to daggerlogs over a game of cards?"

It took the Lady of the House a minute or two before it dawned on her that Willie had mixed up "loggerheads" and "daggers drawn". But she thinks "daggerlogs" is a lovely word and should be in every dictionary!

THE FRIENDSHIP BOOK

GENERATIONS of children have enjoyed the stories that A.A. Milne wrote about his son Christopher Robin. The small boy about whom they were written dearly loved a visit to the theatre with his parents.

Once, he tells us, he was watching Jack Hulbert and Cicely Courtneidge and enjoying himself so much that Cicely noticed him. During the interval she sent round a box of chocolates with the message: "These are for the little boy who is laughing so much."

Whoever we are, actresses or writers, or just husbands and wives, we all need someone to laugh at our jokes, don't we?

DID you know that in winter it can often be warmer outside than in?

A Yorkshire minister kept careful records of temperatures inside and outside his church for one full year. Then he came up with a proposal to reduce heating bills in winter—simply open the church doors!

He had discovered that on mild winter days the outside temperature was often warmer than that inside and leaving the doors open would help to raise the church's inside temperature, besides saving fuel.

It occurred to me that this principle can be applied not only to buildings. If you wrap yourself up in yourself, the chances are that you will feel cold and not at all warm. But if you get outside yourself a bit, have a chat with a neighbour or a shopkeeper, or even with someone in the bus queue, you will feel better and warmer, simply because you've had your doors open to other people!

PERFECTION

When we survey bold Winter's plan,
How trivial seem the works of man.

THE FRIENDSHIP BOOK

I LIKE these simple verses by the Scottish poet and hymnist, Horatius Bonar:-

> Thou must be true thyself,
>   If thou the truth wouldst teach;
> Thy soul must overflow, if thou
>   Another's soul wouldst reach.
> It needs the overflow of heart
>   To give the lips full speech.
>
> Think truly, and thy thoughts
>   Shall the world's famine feed;
> Speak truly, and each word of thine
>   Shall be a fruitful seed;
> Live truly, and thy life shall be
>   A great and noble creed.

THE late Dr William Barclay used to tell a story of a conversation he overheard on the top of a tram. Two women were talking, and one of them was bemoaning how tight her finances were and how she never seemed able to buy the things she would like for the house.

Her friend said that she had taken a part-time job and so had been able to buy a new carpet for the living room.

"Ah, well," was the reply, "but then everything seems to work out well for you — you always were one of the lucky ones."

"Yes, I suppose that's true," the other answered quietly, "though I find that the harder I work, the luckier I seem to be!"

A good story to remember when we tend to blame things on "our bad luck"!

THE FRIENDSHIP BOOK

SOMETIMES we say rather contemptuously of something, "It's not worth a button!" Yet, quite apart from their usefulness, buttons can be very valuable. A collection of antique buttons once fetched several thousand pounds in a London sale-room. And no wonder: there are buttons of silver and gold, of pearl, of carved whalebone, of jet and much besides. Many are intricately decorated.

The inconspicuous things in life are often more precious than we realise. Remember what the biblical prophet said, "Who hath despised the day of small things?"

WHETHER therefore ye eat, or drink, or whatsoever ye do, do all to the glory of God.

1 Corinthians 10, 31

I WONDER how often in the course of a day we use the word "time"? "It's time to get up." "What time is it?" "I've no time." "How time flies!" "We had a marvellous time." "About time, too!"

Time is a bit of a mystery, isn't it? Few of us, I imagine, could define it, but that really doesn't matter as long as we know how to use it.

In his book, "How to Live on Twenty-Four Hours a Day", Arnold Bennett wrote, "Time is the inexplicable raw material of everything; the supply of time is a daily miracle . . . out of it you have to spin health, pleasure, money, content, respect and the evolution of your own immortal soul."

It is worth asking ourselves, "What am I going to spin with the miracle of time today?"

REFLECTING

THE FRIENDSHIP BOOK

BROWSING through my dictionary the other day, I noticed that the first definition given of the word "sound" was "noise". Admittedly it went on to say, "especially a loud or harsh one." I think when we talk of "sound-proofing" we really mean "noise-proofing"! Noises can be a menace, but sounds can be a delight. Who would want to shut out the sound of the song of birds, or the whisper of wind in a forest, the gurgle of a stream, the humming of bees, the lapping of the sea on the beach, or a multitude of other sounds of nature?

There are many other sounds that we wouldn't call a noise—gentle music, the voice of a friend, the singing of a kettle, the bubbling of a pan of soup on the stove. It may sometimes seem to be a harshly noisy world in which we live, but let's be grateful, too, for the hosts of pleasant sounds.

YOU can take it or leave it. Hobson's choice!" You've heard the saying, but who was Hobson? He was a 17th century Cambridge carrier and stable owner who hired out horses and he used to insist that his customers must take the horse nearest the door, not choose the one they preferred. It was a case of "that one — or none at all."

He may have been a bit of an eccentric, but when you think about it, there was good sense behind his system. For one thing, it ensured that none of his horses would be overworked. It also enabled him to avoid being accused of favouritism to any one customer.

The more I think of old Thomas Hobson, the more I feel he had a lot of good, sound commonsense.

B

THE FRIENDSHIP BOOK

MY grandmother was one of the most placid people I have ever met in spite of the heavy burdens she had to bear. Widowed in early middle-age and left with a large family, she was often incapacitated by periods of ill-health. Yet through it all, she preserved a serenity which was the wonder of those who knew her.

She had a simple philosophy which lay behind her quiet cheerfulness, expressed in a verse which she often recited if we were getting a bit upset about anything:

> *For every evil under the sun,*
> *There is a remedy or there is none.*
> *If there is one, try to find it,*
> *If there is none, never mind it.*

I don't think I've ever quite achieved my grandmother's serenity, but the verse has often helped and encouraged me.

OFTEN, when people are seriously ill, or injured in an accident, they are given very special attention in hospital in what is called an "Intensive Care Unit".

A minister, in his magazine, altered this phrase slightly. "I would like this church," he wrote, "to become an Intensive Prayer Unit."

What a difference that could make! Prayer is sometimes a rather formal thing, yet thousands of people have found that, in the words of the poet, Alfred Lord Tennyson,

> *More things are wrought by prayer*
> *Than this world dreams of . . .*

THE FRIENDSHIP BOOK

WE can quote a hundred mottoes,
Give good and wise advice,
We can find a dozen reasons,
Offer arguments precise:
But when it comes to action
And things are getting hot,
We can cut out all the talking
For example beats the lot!

SOME put their trust in chariots, and some in horses: but we will remember the Name of the Lord our God.   Psalm 20, 7

IN an old song, "Green Grow The Rushes, O", we sing, "One is one and all alone, and ever more shall be so."

Often we say, "I am only one; I don't count for much." Well, it is simply not true!

I came across a rather startling "lesson from history" just recently which showed how often just one vote has changed the course of history.

The writer said, "In 1645, one vote gave Oliver Cromwell the control of England, and just four years later, the execution of Charles I took place because of a single vote. Across the Atlantic, in 1776, one vote gave America English instead of German as their language and later, in 1868, one vote saved Andrew Jackson from impeachment. But perhaps the most telling example was that, in 1923, one vote made Adolf Hitler the leader of the Nazi Party."

I am only one. You are only one. But don't let us ever imagine we don't count.

THE FRIENDSHIP BOOK

MARGARET BENTLEY, the Bradford poet, sent me these lovely lines which she has titled "Evening":

> A clean white cloth, a bowl of flowers,
>   The kettle singing while I wait,
> The curtains drawn against the dark,
>   A log fire leaping in the grate.
>
> My senses sharpen as I strain
>   To catch the sounds that say you come,
> The step that brings my heart to life,
>   And makes this empty house my home.

WORDS of sincere, true encouragement are beyond value. Thomas Gray, famous for the poem "Elegy in a Country Churchyard", admitted that he needed it time and time again from his friends.

Even more in need of encouragement was Oliver Goldsmith who was a hack-writer, having tried various other professions, when Dr Samuel Johnson, the famous 18th century literary figure, recognised his great talent. After rescuing him from debt, he encouraged Goldsmith to write plays, one of the most famous of which was " She Stoops To Conquer ".

Encouragement also helped Holman Hunt to paint his most famous religious picture " The Light of the World " now in St Paul's Cathedral, London. With the exception of John Millais, all his friends tried to dissuade him from putting his idea on canvas.

If these great men needed encouragement, how much more is it necesssary to ordinary people? So let's not be sparing with those words of encouragement; they cost nothing, but they can mean so much.

SO WISE

Behind the innocent and playful face
Lies all the wisdom of an ancient race.

THE FRIENDSHIP BOOK

THE young pianist was desperate. He was lonely, hungry, and in debt. He felt so depressed, he tried to kill himself—but failed. In his mortification he went to the piano and got his frustrations out of his system in music.

When he went outside, everything seemed to have taken on a brighter hue. Then it was that he adopted the motto that was to serve him for the rest of his life: "Love life, for better or for worse, without conditions".

Best known perhaps for his playing of Chopin, a fellow-countryman, he is said to have played for more listeners than any other concert pianist in the history of music.

Artur Rubinstein died in his mid-90's, a leading figure in music for over 40 years, and the possessor of a great and fulfilled talent.

THE other day, the Lady of the House took me shopping in the local supermarket — not, I admit, one of my favourite occupations! As we made our way to the check-out, I was leading the way to where there were very few people waiting, but the Lady of the House tugged at my arm and took me to the end of a much longer queue. I looked questioningly at her, but she just put her fingers to her lips.

When we got outside she said, "I know it was a bit longer to wait, but that was my favourite check-out girl. She always has a cheerful word for her customers — it almost makes me forget how expensive everything is!"

Yes, a cheerful word can make all the difference.

THE FRIENDSHIP BOOK

THE little village of Thwaite in North Yorkshire was the home of the two famous nature photographers, Richard and Cherry Kearton. A story is told thereabouts of a member of the Kearton family, a gamekeeper, one of whose chief responsibilities was that of catching trout for his master's table.

When a new master appeared on the scene, Keeper Kearton went down to the river and, as he cast his line, he prayed, " O Lord, if t'new maister's a good 'un, hook 'em on fast. But if he isna', then gie t'trout a chance!"

O REMEMBER not the sins and offences of my youth: but according to thy mercy think thou upon me, O Lord, for thy goodness.   Psalm 25, 7

A JOURNALIST friend of W. Somerset Maugham once visited the great author when he was staying at the Ritz-Carlton hotel in New York. On top of a cabinet in the sumptuous apartment, he noticed an old cracked cup.

His curiosity got the better of him and he asked about it. Somerset Maugham told him that during World War II he had been evacuated from the South of France in a small cargo vessel. Supplies of food and water were very scarce and the passengers had to queue up each day for their meagre rations.

"That cup," he said, "held my daily allowance of water. Whenever I find myself taking the comfortable places I stay in and the good food I eat for granted, I fill up my cup at the tap and drink it—slowly. It brings me to earth again in quite a hurry."

THE FRIENDSHIP BOOK

JOHN'S future seemed very bleak. His father was handicapped and found it difficult to find suitable work in Glasgow. John himself had no proper hands — just stumps. When he was old enough he was sent to a branch of the National Children's Home in the Cotswolds.

In that beautiful countryside, and with lots of love and imagination from those who cared for him, he gained courage. He became a Boy Scout, and even learned to tie knots for which he won badges.

After gaining a scholarship and the correct training, John became a superb artist. His gift lay in illumination. The modest John Buchanan soon had his own studio, and received orders from the Queen. His work is in Liverpool Cathedral, too.

John has had to put a lot of continuing patience and effort into his career and the National Children's Home are very proud of him. Against all odds he has made his life a very splendid thing.

A FRIEND told me of this amusing incident which occurred as she was waiting at a bus stop after being away for a weekend break. An elderly man joined her and, glancing at her travelling bag, asked, "Where are you going?"

"Oh, only a short trip home again," replied my friend.

The old man said gravely, "I'll be going on a long trip soon."

Touched, my friend said, "Well, we all have to take that long trip one day."

He looked at her sharply. "Madam," he retorted, "I'm going to India to visit my son!"

THE FRIENDSHIP BOOK

AMONG all the lovely calendars I have seen, the one that impressed me most was not a big glossy, illustrated one, but a tiny card small enough to go into a wallet or handbag, with the whole year's calendar printed on one side.

It was published by the Royal National Institute for the Blind and was headed simply, " 365 days to appreciate the beauty you can SEE."

THERE is a centuries' old story about an artist who was commissioned to paint a mural in a monastery. At the end of the day the Abbot went to see how the work was progressing, and found the artist sitting gazing at the blank wall in front of him.

At the end of the second day, and of the third, the Abbot found the same thing and by this time he was growing impatient.

"When are you going to start the picture?" he demanded.

"Father," said the artist, "the picture is complete. Tomorrow I start to put it on the wall."

I LOVE the lilt of the Welsh language, and said this to a friend of ours from Anglesey recently, marvelling at the way his tongue got round some of his country's place-names. He smiled at my attempt to say one of them.

"Ah, Francis," he said, "there is an old saying that in order to pronounce Welsh words you need three things: a cold in the head, a twist in the tongue and a husk of barley in the throat!"

So that's the secret of those lovely sounds!

FEBRUARY

SUNDAY—FEBRUARY 1.

UNTO the pure all things are pure.

Titus 1, 15

MONDAY—FEBRUARY 2.

"I LOVE LIFE" is the title of this fine poem sent to me by J. M. Robertson of Edinburgh:

I love life; I love each day,
I love when sunlight starts to stray
Through swaying trees, then pirouettes
Enhancing dancing silhouettes.

I love life; I love the sound
Of feathered friends, who gather round,
And, with each magic melody,
Provide a serenade that's free.

I love life; I love the sight
Of cloud-drifts on a moonlit night.
I love the lap of sea on shore,
And every positive encore.

I love life; I love the kind
Of pleasures that invade the mind;
Of faces, places, moments rare,
So fine and beautiful to share.

I love many other things
The privilege of living brings.
Despite the trouble and the strife,
So much to cherish . . . I love life.

THE FRIENDSHIP BOOK

BUDDHA once came across a group of his monks arguing fiercely on a theological matter. Each believed that he was right, and all the others wrong. Buddha sat down and told them the story of the Rajah, the blind men and the elephant.

One day the Rajah gathered together all the blind men in the town. He then had an elephant brought into their midst. He made one of the blind men touch its ear, another the head, another the trunk, a tusk, the back, the tail, the foot. The Rajah told each one that he was touching an elephant.

When all had felt the elephant, the Rajah said, "Now tell me what an elephant is like." The one who touched the ear said an elephant was like a fan. The one who had touched the head said it was like a pot. For the others—the trunk became a plough; a tusk, a ploughshare; the tail, a pestle; a foot, a pillar; the back, a grain-holder; the tuft of the tail, a besom.

Soon they were all arguing with each other, and saying, "it is like this." "No, it isn't — it's like this!"

"And that," said Buddha quietly, "is what men are like about the truth."

AN old lady, a friend of ours, has a bachelor son whose work takes him all over the world. He never fails to send his mother a card wherever he goes, but the message on it is always very brief. Never more than, "Very hot — John."; "Rain today — John."; "Lovely city — John."

A friend, seeing one of these cards, said, "It doesn't tell you much, does it?"

"Oh, yes it does," smiled the old lady. "It tells me my John is thinking about me!"

THE FRIENDSHIP BOOK

IN his book, "Tennyson, Poet and Prophet", Philip Henderson tells of the Poet Laureate's friendship with an old shepherd who lived near his home. Tennyson himself was then in his seventies and at the height of his fame. He numbered amongst his closest friends many of the greatest in the land, yet he loved nothing better than to slip away of an evening to spend an hour or two in the shepherd's little flint cottage under the northern slope of the High Down.

The shepherd was not the least over-awed by Alfred Tennyson's reputation. When another visitor once read to him from Tennyson's works, the old man remarked, "What a head-piece he must have, and 'ee don't look it, do 'ee?"

And when the old shepherd lay on his deathbed, he told the nurse he would like to talk to Tennyson again before he died. "He is a wonderful man for nature and life."

A fine tribute, and one I am sure Tennyson treasured.

THE minister of a church I used to attend was fond of saying, " You will never be able to *find* time for prayer; you have to *make* time." I never recall those words without also thinking of John Wesley's mother, Susannah, who, with 19 children and her home to manage, still made time for prayer.

It is said that when she wanted to pray amid her busy household she would pull her apron over her face, and the children knew not to disturb their mother when she was " praying into her apron "!

Susannah Wesley is a reminder to us all of the need for, and the possibility of, quietness amid turmoil.

WINTER PEACE

On a glistening, snowy, winter day
The city's bustle seems far away.

THE FRIENDSHIP BOOK

DR EDWARD ROSENOW was a pioneer researcher at the famous Mayo Clinic in New York into the cause and cure of poliomyelitis. He often told how he remembered vividly the moment he decided he wanted to become a doctor.

His brother was seriously ill and the family waited anxiously while the doctor examined him. At last the doctor came back into the room and said, "Don't worry. He's going to get well again."

Rosenow says that he will always remember how his parents' faces lit up with hope. "I decided there and then that I wanted to do the work that could have that effect."

We can't all be doctors, but we can all cause others' faces to light up with a few words of hope, or gratitude or friendly encouragement. It's a great reward to have.

REJOICE with them that do rejoice, and weep with them that weep.   Romans 12, 15

I WONDER what your first thoughts are when you wake up in the morning? I don't doubt that, sometimes at least, there is a bit of apprehension, perhaps even a sigh and a groan: "Monday again!" "Washing day!" — or something of the sort.

In his autobiography, Dr Mervyn Stockwood said that every morning on waking he thought of three things for which he wanted to thank God.

I can't think of a better way to greet the morning, can you?

THE FRIENDSHIP BOOK

IN his book, "Speak For England", Melvyn Bragg has scores of cameos of ordinary life over the last 50 years or so seen through the eyes of people who lived in the little country town of Wigton in Cumbria. They reveal some lovely insights on human nature.

Here is one of them: Mrs Jean Morrison and her husband had lived most of their married life in an attractive, detached house at the edge of the town, on the road to the lakes. From the window of the sitting room they had a glorious view, but it was about to be blocked and hidden by a new housing estate. Mrs Morrison simply said, "We have had the benefit all these years. Now it'll be someone else's turn."

It's a way of looking at life which would help us all to come to terms with its disappointments and frustrations — thankfulness for what we have had, no resentment at what we have lost.

AT the bottom of a flight of stone stairs in an old castle which the Lady of the House and I visited recently was a notice: TAKE CARE — WORN STEPS".

And indeed they were well-worn. By whom, I couldn't help wondering. Soldiers, perhaps, and prisoners; servants; nobles; maybe even kings and queens. Whoever they were, all had left their mark on the hard stone over the years, imperceptible, but all adding up.

The "foot-prints" each of us leaves may seem insignificant yet our lives *do* count and do have an influence. A worn step may not seem a very important memorial, but it is a sign that someone has been there. That *we* have been here is important, too.

THE FRIENDSHIP BOOK

A good friend sent me the transcript of a page from an autograph album compiled during World War I. It is entitled, "A Soldier's Table Of Hymns".

6-30 a.m.: Reveille — "Christians awake".

6-45 a.m.: Rouse Parade — "Art thou weary?".

7-00 a.m.: Breakfast — "Meekly wait and murmur not".

8-15 a.m.: Company Officer's Parade — "When he cometh".

8-45 a.m.: Manoeuvres — "Fight the Good Fight".

11-45 a.m.: Swedish Drill — "Here we suffer grief and pain".

1-00 p.m.: Dinner — "Come, ye thankful people, come".

2-15 p.m.: Rifle Drill — "Go labour on".

3-15 p.m.: Lecture by C.O. — "Tell me the old, old story".

4-30 p.m.: Dismiss — "Praise God from whom all blessings flow".

5-00 p.m.: Tea — "What means this eager, anxious throng?".

6-00 p.m.: "Retreat — "O Lord, how happy we should be".

10-00 p.m.: Last Post — "All are safely gathered in".

10-15 p.m.: Lights Out — "Peace, perfect peace".

THE actress, Diana Rigg, was asked in a television interview about "disasters" in her career, the moments when things went badly wrong. She admitted to one or two, and was then asked, "How long does a disaster last?"

"Oh," she replied, cheefully, "till I get back home. Then a disaster doesn't matter any more."

THE FRIENDSHIP BOOK

HENRY was the seventh of the eight children of a miner. He lived in Castleford, Yorkshire, and like most children in those days he went to Sunday School.

One Sunday afternoon, the superintendent at the school told the children a story about Michelangelo. He told it so well and with such enthusiasm that it seized the imagination of young Henry. He hurried home to read all that he could find about the sculptor. A seed had been sown.

That little boy was Henry Moore, who became one of the greatest of our modern sculptors. Today his work is known and admired throughout the world—and it all started one day in Sunday School.

THE earth is the Lord's, and all that therein is.
Psalm 24, 1

OFTEN we hear stories of jealousy and criticism between people of the same profession, but the greatest never sink to this. I have been reading recently about the novelist Charlotte Brontë and her appreciation of the work of her friendly rival, Mrs Gaskell. Charlotte frequently sent her letters praising her books, but perhaps the height of this generous attitude was reached when she postponed the publication of " Villette " so as not to detract from the appearance of Mrs Gaskell's " Ruth ".

I have always enjoyed Charlotte Brontë's writings, but that story makes them appear in an even better light for me.

C

THE FRIENDSHIP BOOK

A LITTLE while ago the Lady of the House and I were looking round a folk museum at Llangollen in North Wales. We were particularly interested in some of the farmhouse lore. Superstitious much of it may have been, but we couldn't help feeling that there was a lot of wisdom in an old notice which read: "You must never make a noise in a dairy because milk likes peace and is sure to curdle if it is jarred or has clumsy folk about."

True? I really don't know, but I *do* know that life itself would be a lot sweeter if there was a bit more gentleness and quietness about.

JEAN FORREST of Cleveland wrote this amusing poem about that eternal mystery, the British weather:

I wake to a day that is cloudy and grey,
So I put on my hat and my mac.
I walk down the street with my boots on my feet,
And the crafty old sun's creeping back.
I run to the house as fast as a mouse,
And quickly change into a dress,
But before I can go I hear thunder and so,
I'm getting confused I confess.
I creep out the door and slip on the floor
When I find there is snow on the ground.
I walk into a tree, it's not easy to see
When the fog is so thick all around.
It just seems to me, and I'm sure you agree,
That our crazy old weather's unique.
Where else would you find, snow, rain, sun and
*   wind—*
Not yearly, but all in one week!

THE FRIENDSHIP BOOK

THE great evangelist Gypsy Smith used to tell a story about when his daughter was small. He had been on a long tour and the day after his return they went together to a bazaar. Everybody was wanting to speak to him and hear the story of his travels. In the crush, his little girl tried hard to cling to his hand. At last he bent down and pressed a coin into her hand. " Here Zillah," he said, " Take this and go and buy yourself something."

Zillah's mouth puckered up and her eyes filled with tears. " Daddy," she sobbed, " I don't want your old money—*I want you.*"

It was a lesson he never forgot.

THE late Sir Compton Mackenzie, the famous writer, was always fascinated by islands and spent many years of his life on them — Capri, Herm, Jethou and Barra among them.

He said that his very first "island" was a large hearthrug on which he and his friends played when small — trying hard not to put their legs over the edge in case they were bitten by sharks! Towards the end of his life, when he had to spend much of his day in bed — a magnificent green and gold Venetian four-poster — he used to call it, "my last island."

It's the sort of imaginative idea one might expect from a writer, and yet, though companionship should form an important part of our lives there is a place, too, for quiet "islands" of solitude — an armchair, a corner of the garden, a seat in the park — where we can be still and retreat for a little from the bustle of life. I have my own imaginative "island" of quietness; I hope you have, too.

THE FRIENDSHIP BOOK

<u>SATURDAY—FEBRUARY 21.</u>

I DON'T think I ever see a child with an old teddy bear without recalling a story I heard many years ago of a small girl who went into hospital to have her tonsils out. She took with her a rather worn, one-eyed teddy bear and she was clutching him tightly as the time came for her to be taken to the operating theatre.

"I think you should leave Teddy there," said the surgeon gently. "I will have a look at him, too, while he's here."

And when the little girl came round after the operation she found Teddy at her side, with a tiny bandage across his missing eye — that kindly surgeon's very own work!

<u>SUNDAY—FEBRUARY 22.</u>

APPLY thine heart unto instruction, and thine ears to the words of knowledge.   Proverbs 23, 12

<u>MONDAY—FEBRUARY 23.</u>

IVAN TURGENEV, the famous Russian novelist, once saw a ragged, down-and-out beggar in the street. He stopped beside the man intending to give him some money, but to his embarrassment, as he searched his pockets he found he had not a single coin.

He grasped the beggar's outstretched hand and said, with real regret in his voice, "I'm terribly sorry, but I haven't anything to give you."

"Never mind," said the beggar, "but thank you for this — your handshake is a gift worth having."

How rich we are if we can give friendship, a smile, a handshake, encouragement, good cheer, sympathy. These are gifts indeed.

THE FRIENDSHIP BOOK

WE have many ways of greeting people — shaking hands, embracing, kissing, saluting. In parts of Tibet there is still an ancient and curious form of greeting — people hold out their hands with open palms, and stick out their tongues!

The open hand shows that no weapon is concealed, and the tongue (which, anciently, was supposed to be black if a person was evil) shows that only words of welcome, kindness and truth will be spoken.

We would certainly get curious, even indignant, looks if we tried out this greeting on people we met, but it goes to show that all over the world, friendly hands and friendly words are the way to happy relationships.

CAROL WILLS sent me a number of fine poems from her pen. I enjoyed all of them, but this one in particular makes me want to give that little bit extra:

> *Today I'll try much harder, Lord,*
> *To do the things I ought,*
> *I really will endeavour*
> *To dwell on purer thought.*
>
> *I'll try to speak more kindly, Lord,*
> *To all the folk I meet,*
> *And show more loving kindness*
> *With heart sincerely sweet.*
>
> *But when you look my way, Lord,*
> *And my efforts are unveiled,*
> *I pray you too will try, Lord,*
> *To forget the times I failed.*

FRIENDS

THE FRIENDSHIP BOOK

THE playwright, Christopher Morley, once wrote, " When you sell a man a book you don't sell him just twelve ounces of paper and ink and glue—you sell him a whole new life."

Whether we possess a library or just a handful of books, I imagine most of us know what Morley meant. Books introduce us to new places, new people, new ideas and experiences.

Charles Lamb used to say that he thought we ought to say grace for books as well as for food. How about taking out your favourite book and doing just that today?

AS her contribution to the local Sunday School Open Night, the Lady of the House agreed to organise a Children's Bible quiz.

She tried to make the questions reasonably easy but was prepared to receive some unusual answers. However, I think even she was surprised when, in answer to the question, "What is an epistle?" one small boy answered confidently, "The wife of an apostle"!

IN his book "How To Stop Worrying and Start Living", Dale Carnegie tells the story of the development of the motor car tyre. The first ones, he tells us, were made to *resist* shock and they were cut to pieces. Then they made tyres to *absorb* the shock and *they* stood up to the strain.

Isn't that a parable of life? It's when we accept the shocks of life and take them in our stride, rather than just let these things buffet us, that we learn the secret of victorious living.

MARCH

SUNDAY—MARCH 1.

A ND he changeth the times and the seasons: he removeth kings, and setteth up kings: he giveth wisdom unto the wise, and knowledge to them that know understanding.   Daniel 2, 21

MONDAY—MARCH 2.

IT pays to be on the right track, doesn't it? Sometimes even famous tourists have gone astray.

It is told that when Harriet Beecher Stowe, the author of "Uncle Tom's Cabin", visited Scotland she gazed in awe at what she believed to be Bothwell Bridge, trying to re-picture the famous battle. Later, she was told that she had been looking at the wrong bridge.

Something similar occurred when Nathaniel Hawthorne visited the English Lake District. He gazed with wonder at what he thought was William Wordsworth's house, then discovered that it was the wrong dwelling.

A friend of mine did something similar when hunting for "Little Nell's" gravestone in Tong churchyard. Little Nell is a character in Charles Dickens's novel, "The Old Curiosity Shop" and he had heard that there was a gravestone in her honour in Tong churchyard. Only instead of being Tong in Yorkshire where my friend looked, the stone is at Tong in Shropshire!

Life's a bit like that. It is a track and sometimes we miss our way, or look in the wrong direction. The wonderful thing is that we can always retrace our steps, find the right road and set out again.

THE FRIENDSHIP BOOK

YOU can almost hear the wind in the trees in these lines by Miriam Eker:

I like a billowy, blowy day,
When the wind goes sweeping by,
A rollicking, roisterous, roaring day
That makes the cobwebs fly;
A day that takes me off my feet,
And sets my hat awry,
The keenest, cleanest kind of day,
With which no others vie.
You may have your balmy, gentle days,
But those for which I sigh
Are the wild and wilful windy days
That lift my spirits high.

THERE is an old legend of a father who sent his three sons up a mountain, to see what they could find.

The first didn't get very high up the mountain, but brought back a bunch of flowers. The second climbed higher and found beautiful stones containing precious minerals. The third son returned empty- handed, but his face was aglow with happiness. "I climbed to the top of the mountain where there was nothing except bare rock. But Father—I saw the sea!"

The others brought back something *in their hands.* He brought something *in his mind.* Of course possessions are important, but seeing is often more precious than having. An ancient cathedral, a costly work of art, a stately home, a concert by a great orchestra, a lovely forest—few of us can *possess* these things, but how rich we are if we have them in our minds!

THE FRIENDSHIP BOOK

THE other day the Lady of the House and I took some visitors to our local airport to watch the arrivals and departures of planes large and small.

As we watched these marvellous pieces of engineering I couldn't help recalling a cutting from a newspaper article which I filed away many years ago. It talked of "the chilly December day when two shivering mechanics from Dayton, Ohio, first felt their homemade contraption, whittled out of hickory sticks, gummed together with Arnstein's bicycle cement, stretched with muslin they'd sewn on their sister's sewing-machine in their own backyard, soar into the air above the dunes".

The two were, of course, the famous Wright brothers. Surely we should, now and again, pause and recall how much we owe not only to the skill but the patience and vision of all those people who have been pioneers in so many spheres and have given us things which nowadays we take so much for granted.

FRIDAY—MARCH 6.

WHEN the writer J. M. Barrie was a young man in London it was a tradition that journalists should wear tall hats, especially when visiting important editors. Barrie and another equally poor young man shared a room—and a hat, as they had only one old one between them. Whoever was going to visit an editor wore it. Greenwood was the name of the editor they visited most frequently so they christened it "The Greenwood Hat"!

Sir James Barrie used to tell this story with a twinkle in his eye, but of course there is a lesson in the story, for sharing, whether it be possessions or news, makes life richer both for ourselves and others.

THE FRIENDSHIP BOOK

A FRIEND of ours has a tiny country cottage which is very primitive and sparsely furnished, but a marvellous place for " getting away from it all ".

He and his wife invited the Lady of the House and me to stay there with them for a weekend, and as we were retiring to our room for the night he said, " If you find yourself short of anything, let us know. We can show you how to do without it!"

That, of course, was his joking way of half-apologising for the simplicity of our surroundings, but isn't it a good thing sometimes to try and detach ourselves a little from some of the material things which have become so much part of our lives?

I must say, we enjoyed our experience of the simple life and came away refreshed.

C AST thy bread upon the waters: for thou shalt find it after many days.   Ecclesiastes 11, 1

I T is said that Raphael, the 15th century Italian painter, used to wear a candle in a specially-made cap so that when he was painting, his shadow would not fall upon his work.

This period of Lent, leading up to the great festival of Easter, has always been observed by Christians as a time of self-sacrifice. The story of Raphael reminds us how easy it is, even in our service for others, to let the shadow of selfishness, of self-interest fall on what we do.

It's hard to forget ourselves — yet that, in part at least, is what Lent is all about.

THE FRIENDSHIP BOOK

TUESDAY—MARCH 10.

WE heard recently from our friend Jill who moved, not long ago, into a charming, Victorian end-of-terrace house. She had fallen in love with the house and got on well with the friendly neighbours, but there was a problem which threatened to spoil it all. In stormy weather the wind howls along the alley at the side of the house, and the awful noise made her very nervous.

Jill tried keeping extra busy in bad weather, and often played her radio loudly in an effort to combat the noise. She even tried ear-plugs. Then one day, she decided to face her problem head-on. She went and sat in the noisiest room and *listened* to the wind. As she did so, she became aware that it was making a strange kind of music. Soon she had completely forgotten the gale blowing outside. She was too busy enjoying her new harpsichord sounds.

Of course, there was a simply explanation. What Jill heard was the sound of the wind playing through the telephone wires. But doesn't it illustrate how easy it is to tackle our fears and conquer them?

WEDNESDAY—MARCH 11.

SIR THOMAS LIPTON, who founded the huge chain of grocery stores, believed that one of the most valuable things in life was laughter.

In many of his early stores he had two mirrors—a concave one as you went in, and a convex one as you came out. Thus, as you entered the store you saw yourself looking thin and hungry, and as you left you saw yourself short, fat and happy.

Good for trade? Well, perhaps so. But good for the customer, too. All praise to those who can make us smile and laugh at ourselves.

THE FRIENDSHIP BOOK

HAVE you heard of the "Road of the Loving Heart"? It is fringed with palm trees and leads through the beautiful island of Samoa. The Samoan chiefs who built it had all been released from jail thanks to the efforts of the writer Robert Louis Stevenson who spent the last few years of his life on the island.

Grateful to him for their release, the chiefs built this special road, and placed an inscription at the corner:

"Remembering the great love of his highness Tusitala, and his loving care when we were in prison and sore distressed, we have prepared him an enduring present, this road which we have dug to last for ever."

And so Stevenson, known to the Samoans as Tusitala, the Teller of Tales, is still remembered by all who travel the "Road of the Loving Heart".

HAVE you ever lain awake at night worrying about something? Of course you have. Next time you do, think of these lines by Marjorie Stiling of Exmouth, Devon. They say what we all know to be true:

> *Thoughts that claim the tired mind*
> *By night, loom black; from all*
> *Their true proportions creep*
> *Before they fade.*
> *Take heart,*
> *For when dawn breaks you'll find*
> *Your spirits soothed, and all*
> *Those doubts and fears grown small;*
> *HOPE — born of sleep.*

THE FRIENDSHIP BOOK

SATURDAY—MARCH 14.

THE actress, Wendy Craig, has said that one of her most vivid war-time memories as a small girl was that of watching her grandmother, who was blind, sitting knitting khaki squares to be made into blankets for the Forces. As she knitted, she quietly sang some of the children's hymns familiar to her from school assemblies during her years as a headmistress.

Wendy says that often, when she feels tense and frustrated, she thinks back to that tranquil scene all these years ago.

I am sure we can all conjure up such pictures of tranquillity if we try; and what a blessing they can be to us!

SUNDAY—MARCH 15.

HE revealeth the deep and secret things: he knoweth what is in the darkness, and the light dwelleth with him.   Daniel 2, 22

MONDAY—MARCH 16.

A SCHOOLMASTER of my boyhood days used to say, if anybody complained that a certain subject was boring, "There is no such thing as a boring subject — only people who are bored!"

I was reminded of this recently when someone talking on television about the diarist Samuel Pepys, said "His diary is so fascinating because Pepys was never bored. He was just as interested in the price of vegetables as in what the king or a duke said about some national problem."

Nor need *we* be bored today. For, as Robert Louis Stevenson reminds us:

The world is so full of a number of things,
I'm sure we should all be as happy as kings.

THE CALL

No four-post bed for the son who's bred
To answer the sea-bird's call,
But the canopy high of a starry sky
And the sway of a masthead tall.

THE FRIENDSHIP BOOK

GUSTAVE EIFFEL, the famous French engineer, once said of the great tower in Paris which perpetuates his name, "I should really be jealous of the tower. People seem to think it is my only work, but I have done many other things, too."

He had, indeed. Long before the tower he had revolutionised bridge-building by making sectional wrought-iron bridges. At first his critics waited for them to fall down! When they didn't, they were copied by others all over Europe.

Eiffel never resented the copying of his designs and ideas. He used to say that what had given him pleasure in conceiving ought to give others pleasure in making and use. "Besides," he would add, "I can always invent something else!"

We know he was a great engineer, but that remark shows that he was also a man with a great heart and mind.

IT must be hard for a writer who has to live with her critics: even when the critics are pint-sized and wearing bunny-rabbit pyjamas.

Our friend Angie, who is a children's writer, says she'll never forget the time she received her first "review". It was bedtime and her three small children sat and dutifully listened as she read aloud one of her own stories published in an annual.

"Well, did you like it?" she asked, as she closed the book.

The three sat and thought for a moment. Then the youngest boy piped up as spokesman. "It was a jolly good story, Mum, but next time can we please have a *real* one?"

THE FRIENDSHIP BOOK

I LISTENED recently to a sermon on the familiar parable of the talents, dealing particularly with the man who had only one — symbolising, the preacher said, ordinary people like most of us.

A sentence from that sermon has remained in my mind since I heard it: "A little thing is a little thing; but faithfulness in little things is a very great thing."

Now, that's worth remembering.

THERE'S nothing older people like better than to talk of former times — the interests and experiences they had as children and young adults.

Sometimes younger people tend to weary a little of these old tales. Recently, though, I came across a young farmer's wife who just loves to collect information on the past from older people. It all started when she was asked to give an illustrated talk about changes in the area. Her interest snowballed from there.

Groups of elderly people invited her to their meetings. Many of them brought along old postcards and photographs to show her. These "treasures" they were often generous enough to lend so that she could add to local knowledge of the district.

She is not alone in this interest in the past. Other men and women pursue it. And at a time when so much of Britain is changing, such "then and now" topics are important. Older people have a heritage of memories which needs to be gleaned and treasured.

More often than not, this results in "two way traffic" as is experienced in so many aspects of life. The more interest is shown, the wider these interests become.

D

THE FRIENDSHIP BOOK

FEW artists painted clouds more beautifully and realistically than John Constable, yet probably few people know the story behind this.

His parents intended him to be a clergyman, but when he showed no aptitude, he was put to work in one of his father's flour mills. He found the work hard and unsatisfying, but the time he spent there brought unexpected results.

Working in a windmill he was very dependent upon the weather. He was continually watching the clouds for signs of a favourable wind. John Constable found this a fascinating study. He learned which clouds brought rain, or hail or sleet and he observed the variety and changing colours of clouds — all knowledge which he was to use in his great and well-loved landscape paintings.

AND all things, whatsoever ye shall ask in prayer, believing, ye shall receive.   Matthew 21, 22

DID you hear about the group of Roman soldiers who attacked a Christian church because they had heard that it contained some valuables? The Roman officer called the priest to him and commanded: "Show me your treasures."

The priest did not reply at once, but took the officer to a room behind the church, in which the sick were being looked after, the poor were being given food and clothing, and widows and orphans were resting.

"There," said the priest. "These are the treasures of my church."

THE FRIENDSHIP BOOK

MY niece Joanna, who was staying with us for the weekend, asked me to take her to the park. I agreed, although I had had other plans for the morning.

While Joanna chased her ball I thought about the weeding, the sagging gate and a peeling window that were all awaiting my attention.

"Come on, Uncle Francis! Let's play catch," Joanna shouted, throwing her ball my way, and I forgot about the jobs that were undone.

That whole weekend I relaxed and enjoyed my young niece's company. The jobs would get done eventually, but meanwhile Joanna was growing up fast so it was important to enjoy her company while she was still a child.

When her father came to fetch her, Joanna's first words were, "I *have* enjoyed the weekend, Daddy. Uncle Francis took me to the park and we had a lovely time together."

A wasted weekend? Never!

YEARS ago a young American, Mary McCracken, was completely crippled in her legs as a result of infantile paralysis. She longed to take up a medical career, but was refused permission to enter the American colleges to which she applied because they said she would never be able to practise.

Undeterred, she went to China, took her medical degree at Peking University where she was top of her class and came back to Philadelphia where she had been refused training. There she took up work in a hospital for crippled children—practising from a wheelchair.

THE FRIENDSHIP BOOK

THURSDAY—MARCH 26.

VISITING my doctor's surgery recently I was amused by the comment of a man sitting opposite me in the waiting room. Looking at his watch he shook his head gloomily and said, "I have been here over an hour now. No wonder we are called 'patients'!"

FRIDAY—MARCH 27.

I DON'T know who said it, but truly it was worth saying:
"Gentleness is the gift of the gods: nothing is so strong as gentleness, and nothing is so gentle as real strength."

SATURDAY—MARCH 28.

TOMORROW is Mothering Sunday when children and adults alike will be thinking of their mothers and showing their love and appreciation in all sorts of different ways. Here is how the poet Fay Inchfawn put it in her poem "For This And More":

> *For all your patient care;*
> *For every anguished prayer;*
> *For every gentle look;*
> *For every step you took;*
> *For every anxious night;*
> *For every kindly light;*
> *For tact with awkward ways;*
> *For love on wayward days;*
> *For hope when there was none;*
> *For faith when hope was done;*
> *For all you ever thought;*
> *For all you ever wrought;*
> *Today, and now, and here,*
> *I thank you, Mother dear.*

SWINGING

Look at me swinging high —
This must be how it feels to fly!

THE FRIENDSHIP BOOK

H E maketh the barren woman to keep house, and be the joyful mother of children. Psalm 113, 9

W HEN Sir Wilfred Grenfell, the intrepid missionary to Labrador, was a boy, he was sent from his Cheshire home in Parkgate to be a boarder at Marlborough College in Wiltshire.

It was the custom there for the boys to wear a flower in their buttonholes at the school chapel service on Sunday mornings, and Grenfell told how his mother faithfully sent this to him every week. It was an act which made a deep impression on him and one he always remembered.

One of his biographers, W.J. Smart, says, "He pictured her at home, so many miles away in Parkgate, with the thousand worries of his father's boarding school whose business side she largely managed, making time to pick, pack and post that token of her love, and it gave him a lifelong appreciation of flowers."

And, I would add, of his mother.

S INCE I first heard them many years ago I have never forgotten the words of this Chinese proverb:

If there is righteousness in the heart, there will be beauty in the character. If there be beauty in the character, there will be harmony in the home. If there be harmony in the home, there will be order in the nation. When there is order in the nation, there will be peace in the world.

Truly there is wisdom in the East.

APRIL

WEDNESDAY—APRIL 1.

THERE is an old story from the days of sail of sailors who hailed a passing ship and asked for water as they had run out and were dying of thirst.

"Water?" came the reply from the other ship. "Let down your buckets. There is water there and to spare!"

It was true, for, without knowing it, they had entered the estuary of a great river and were surrounded by fresh water.

Life is like that. We are surrounded by infinite resources of which sometimes we seem quite unaware — friendship, music, books, the beauty of the world of Nature, great pictures, stately buildings — this is only to touch the fringe of all the good things about us upon which we can draw if we will. What a pity we sometimes deprive ourselves of the refreshment they can give.

THURSDAY—APRIL 2.

A FEW weeks ago, I bumped into our friend, Beryl. She told me of the time her husband took her and the family out to dinner at a well-known restaurant, as a special treat.

"For many weeks," Beryl said, "I had been trying to improve the family's table manners, and as usual snapped out, 'Elbows!' when I saw them all slouching over their plates."

She felt embarrassed when she remembered where she was, but admitted that she was even more embarrassed when all round the restaurant everyone guiltily shot up straight!

THE FRIENDSHIP BOOK

SIR NORMAN ANGELL, the economist, once introduced his friend, Harold Wright, to a group of people by saying, "This is Harold. He doesn't do anything—he just *is*."

It isn't recorded what Harold said, but I hope he took the words for the compliment they were certainly meant to be.

Of course, it is important that there should be people in the world who *do* things, but with the emphasis we put on achievements don't let's overlook the people who just *are*—and are friendly, trustworthy, patient, tolerant and sympathetic.

Perhaps it's better to be these things than to do many of the things by which the world sets such store. I'm grateful for the people I know who "just are!"

SATURDAY—APRIL 4.

YET another charity appeal had dropped through our letter-box. The Lady of the House picked it up, read it through in silence and then, holding it out, said, "Francis, there's no arguing with this one, is there?"

The senders had added this little verse to their letter:

"What! Giving again?" I ask in dismay.
"And must I keep giving and giving away?"
"Oh, no," said the angel, looking me through,
"Just keep giving till the Master stops giving to you!"

SUNDAY—APRIL 5.

BEHOLD I stand at the door, and knock: if any man hear my voice, and open the door, I will come in to him.   Revelations 3, 20

THE FRIENDSHIP BOOK

THE late Agatha Christie, writer of many detective stories, made the following comment in a letter to a correspondent: "I assure you the world is really a good and very interesting place. But to enjoy sunlight one has to notice the shadows."

Someone else has pointed out that "it does not pay to live in gloomy shadows when there is so much bright sunshine in the world."

Whilst the American author M. B. Whitman advised: "Keep your face always towards the sunshine and the shadows will fall behind you."

MANY of us who watch gardening programmes on television must sometimes be reduced not merely to envy but sometimes to near despair when we compare our own results with what the experts achieve.

A programme presenter, Geoff Hamilton, walked round the famous North Yorkshire gardens of Newby Hall with one of the staff and remarked on one clump of plants very much taller than the surrounding ground cover plants.

The gardener smiled a little ruefully. "Yes," he said, "I am afraid that is a mistake. We didn't read our instructions carefully enough and didn't expect it to grow so tall."

"Ah, well," said Geoff Hamilton, "it is a bit of a comfort to know that even the experts don't get it right every time!"

I certainly take comfort from that — not only for my garden but for lots of other disappointments, too. We can't be right all the time — and shouldn't expect to be!

THE FRIENDSHIP BOOK

WHEN Mrs Smith was made redundant after 40 years working at the local mill, it seemed as if the bottom had dropped out of her world and at first she was quite depressed.

And then she stopped to take stock of herself. Her husband wasn't at all well, and now she'd have more time to spend with him; she knew lots of folk confined to their homes because of illness or age — she'd have more time to visit them; her little chapel needed extra pairs of hands to clean and dust — she would be free to help there.

Three years later when I asked how she was finding life she smiled and said, "I've so much to do, I don't know how I ever found time to work! I'm counting my blessings and grateful that I'm able to lend a hand where it's needed."

Many folk bless the day when Mrs Smith was made redundant — because now she has so much time to give to others.

THIS is an old poem I came across years ago and have never forgotten because it shows the importance of little things:

The smallest crust may save a human life;
The smallest act may lead to human strife;
The smallest touch may cause the body pain;
The smallest spark may fire a field of grain;
The smallest deed may tell the truly brave;
The smallest skill may serve a life to save;
The smallest drop the thirsty may relieve;
The slightest shock may make a heart to grieve.
Nought is so small that it may not contain
The rose of pleasure — or the thorn of pain.

PURE GOLD

After the rigours of Winter,
Oh, the pleasure that colour can bring!
Transparent and gold, a joy to behold;
Quite suddenly — it's Spring!

THE FRIENDSHIP BOOK

THE other day I was sitting quietly in the local park with a friend, chatting and admiring the surrounding beauty.

But two old men on an adjoining seat were not having such a peaceful time. They had managed to become engaged in a rather acrimonious discussion.

My friend nudged me, winked and said, " Do you hear all that? It bears out a remark I read in a magazine recently: ' An argument is two people trying to get the last word in first!' "

A FRIEND of ours has a beautiful passion flower plant in his greenhouse. I had long been familiar with the way some of the features of the flower have been said to represent aspects of Christ's crucifixion — the corona symbolising the crown of thorns; the five-lobed leaves and curling tendrils representing the hands and scourges of those who flogged Jesus; the five petals and sepals signifying the 10 apostles (Peter who denied Jesus and Judas who betrayed Him being omitted); the three stigmas standing for the nails.

Now a friend has added to this list. The shape of the flower reminds him of the star which led the Wise Men to Jesus; the colour of the petals, he says, exactly matches the traditional colour of the Virgin Mary's dress, while the fact that the plant is a vine recalls the first miracle — the turning of water into wine at Canaan.

MANY waters cannot quench love, neither can the floods drown it.   Song of Solomon 8, 7

THE FRIENDSHIP BOOK

EDWARD BORLAND RAMSAY calls this his "Spring Prayer".

> *Lord, bless the Spring,*
> *The birds that sing*
> *Thy songs of praise;*
> *The thoughtful showers*
> *That make the flowers*
> *So petal-wise;*
> *They thank Thee, Lord,*
> *Each eventide*
> *In humble prayer,*
> *And so may we*
> *In such things see*
> *Thy presence there.*

IT is sometimes said that "it is deeds not words that count," and while I understand what lies behind that saying I don't think we should under-estimate the importance of words. Nor am I thinking simply of the stirring utterances of statesmen, preachers and public speakers of all kinds which must have moved and influenced most of us at some time or other during our lives.

I am thinking also of simple words of kindness, sympathy, encouragement, humour and happiness which it is in the power of all of us to utter. That is why I like the words of the American poet, Emily Dickinson:

> *A word is dead*
> *When it is said,*
> *Some say.*
> *I say it just*
> *Begins to live*
> *That day.*

THE FRIENDSHIP BOOK

FRED, an old friend of ours, has been crippled with rheumatism for many years, but he never lets it get him down. When people ask him how he is, he will invariably reply, " Well, I have my good days and my bad days, but not to worry, I find the good days cancel out the bad ones!"

If only we could all learn to let the good in life cancel out the bad, how much happier we should be.

THE Forth Rail Bridge was the most famous bridge in the world when it was completed, and it must be on record as the greatest pioneering work ever to be undertaken by engineers. The lessons learned while it was being built are still used by industry today.

Did you know that the bridge "grows" with heat expansion? On a hot summer's day it may measure two metres more than on a cold winter day. It took seven years to build, which meant pain and sweat for the shift-workers and new giant-size problems for the designers, but when it was finished it was a marvel to behold. Neither clumsy nor fragile, it was an original creation of interlaced strength and beauty.

What was the secret of the building of the Forth Bridge? Recently I was speaking to a engineer who told me that in steel construction work, a light framework of lengths of steel is even stronger than heavy columns and beams. No length of steel in a framework is unloaded at any time, each member taking its share of the stresses and so the framework acts as one powerful body.

Surely there is a parallel here with our everyday living.

THE FRIENDSHIP BOOK

OVER 200 years ago, a rich young German count, Nicholas von Zinzendorf, drove into Dusseldorf and, leaving his horses to be groomed at the inn, he strolled around the town. Entering the art gallery, he glanced casually at the pictures until he came to one by Stenberg of the Crucifixion. Underneath it was written:

All this I did for thee,
What hast thou done for Me?

He stood strangely captivated by the picture, hour after hour, oblivious of the coming and going of other visitors, until an attendant touched his arm and announced that the gallery was about to close.

That chance visit altered the whole course of his life, for it led him to devote his energies and his wealth to the work of the Moravian Church. The Count von Zinzendorf was one of the many thousands who have seen Good Friday as a life-changing, world-changing force.

MANY years ago, Dr Alexander J. Grieve was Principal of a Congregational training college for ministerial students. One of the things he strongly disliked in services of worship, and against which he advised his students, was the shortening of hymns by missing out one or two of the verses.

He used to snort indignantly, "Saving two minutes on the brink of eternity!" A reminder to us, I think, that time isn't everything!

HE is not here: for he is risen, as he said. Come, see the place where the Lord lay.   Mark 28, 6

THE FRIENDSHIP BOOK

SAMUEL CLEMENS, better known as the author, Mark Twain, had a period in his life when he engaged in a long and almost frantic search for evidence of life after death. He visited libraries and bookshops reading every work on the subject which he could lay hands on.

At length, sadly putting down one of the books, he said to his housekeeper, "It's no good. I can't believe it — I just can't believe it!"

"Mr Clemens," was the reply, "you *do* believe it. You wouldn't have spent all that time reading those books if you didn't."

Surely a thought worth pondering as, at this Easter season, the Church proclaims its victorious message of life after death.

I'VE said it before, but make no apology for saying it again: a letter from a friend is a wonderful tonic. Here is how Mrs Birchall of Warfield, near Bracknell, Berkshire, puts it in a letter to me:

Why not put pen to paper, and write someone a letter,
And if they're feeling ill or sad, 'twill help them to feel better?
The telephone is useful, on this we all depend,
But nothing really matches a letter from a friend,
With little bits of gossip, and news of every kind,
The arrival of a grandson are the things that spring to mind;
So when you have an hour to spare, just give a thought or two
To friends who would appreciate, a letter just from you.

HAVEN

E

THE FRIENDSHIP BOOK

G. F. WATTS, the painter, went for a walk one starlit night with a young man whose behaviour was giving concern to some of his friends. They had asked Watts (known for his understanding and sympathy) if he would talk to the lad and see if he could help.

The encounter *did* have a beneficial effect on the young man who determined to pull himself together and make a fresh start. When he was asked later what happened on the walk to bring about the great change in his attitude, he said simply, "We talked about the stars."

How helpful it is sometimes to be taken right outside our own little personal problems and to contemplate something greater than ourselves.

A FRIEND who has much to do with organising playgroups for children under school age was telling me of her golden rule when visiting a new group. It's just this: Never leave without saying at least one complimentary thing.

The organisation may be bad. The organisers may resent advice and think they know how everything should be done. But however wrong you think they may be, always say one nice thing, even if it's only to admire a scarf somebody is wearing or to pay a compliment about a picture on the wall.

What you say may be quite unimportant, but there's nothing worse than going away leaving an impression that you didn't find anything to praise.

We may say we don't care if people don't notice the kind or clever things we do, but deep down don't we all yearn to be appreciated?

THE FRIENDSHIP BOOK

A SMALL boy, out shopping with his mother, was just at the stage in his reading when he enjoyed reciting aloud the signs and posters which he saw in the shop windows.

They stopped in front of a travel agency and a poster filled him with amazement.

"Mummy, look," he said, " 'Canaries — £356!' How much did our budgie cost?"

ONE of the most attractive and popular Sunday School papers in the 1930's was entitled "Sunbeam". To be a Sunbeam 50 years ago, you had to accept this pledge:

"In order to promote happiness, efficiency, and civic welfare, I sincerely promise that wherever I am:

I will talk health instead of sickness;

I will talk prosperity instead of failure;

I will carry good news instead of bad news;

I will tell the cheerful tale instead of the sad tale;

I will mention blessings instead of my burdens;

I will speak of the sunshine instead of the clouds;

I will think of the cheerful things, not the gloomy, and my thoughts will shine in my face;

I will praise, whenever I can, those who are putting forth an honest effort to perform their tasks creditably;

I will always remember: a merry heart doeth good like a medicine."

SEEK ye the Lord while he may be found, call ye upon him while he is near.   Isaiah 55, 6

MORNING BRIGHT

Up, off and out in the blue of the dawning,
Perfect companions on four feet and two.
Think what they're missing, those lie-a-beds, yawning!
Now, where will we go, and what will we do?

THE FRIENDSHIP BOOK

MONDAY—APRIL 27.

MADAME JULIE RECAMIER lived from 1777 to 1849 and has gone down in history as "the perfect listener". Her portrait, by the French painter, David, hangs in the Louvre in Paris. The expression on her face is one of serene calm — the lips are closed ready to smile, the eyes gaze sympathetically at the beholder.

It is said that when Napoleon first met her, he was so captivated that he forgot what he was going to say. The Duke of Wellington was also lost for words in her presence.

Madame Recamier was obviously a charming person and in his painting of her, the artist captured her incomparable gift, that of being the perfect listener.

TUESDAY—APRIL 28.

I KNOW a young minister who likes to bring home a lesson to youngsters by practical example.

Recently he told the Sunday school about the folly of judging by appearances. It's what's inside that matters, he said.

Then he asked some children to step forward. Each of them was invited to take a chocolate dainty from a box. But there weren't enough to go round and one boy was left with — an onion!

Needless to say, he was somewhat taken aback, but his disappointment changed to curiosity when the minister handed him a knife and asked him to cut the vegetable.

The boy cut it and in the middle found — a 50 pence piece.

I'm sure the lesson will be with him for a long time to come.

THE FRIENDSHIP BOOK

A YOUNG Scottish officer was carrying a bag containing all the money which was shortly to be paid to his company. It was a windy day and getting out of his car he picked up the bag by the wrong end; suddenly the air was full of notes blowing all over the parade ground.

From every barrack block, soldiers ran out and chased the flying money, while the young officer went in to his company commander and reported the disaster.

He got very little sympathy. As he was calculating how long it would take him to pay back the missing money, a message boy delivering meat to the barracks came to him with a handful of crumpled notes. Then, one by one, soldiers came into the office with notes. They were smoothed out and counted, until at last it was announced to the company officer, "Every penny is accounted for, sir."

The young officer in the story became Sir Bernard Fergusson, who was to win renown as a commander in Burma. He told the story to illustrate how loyal the members of a company would be to an officer they held in regard. I think it also shows that there are more honest people in the world than we sometimes believe.

D ID you hear about the Sunday-school teacher in York who talked to her class about " repentance "? When summing up, she asked what was the first essential before we could expect forgiveness.

A little boy's hand shot up. " Please, Miss—we must sin!"

MAY

FRIDAY—MAY 1.

THERE are still a few close-knit country communities in England where the old forms of address " thee " and " thou " are used between members of a family and close friends. However, it is frowned upon if " outsiders " use these terms. One such " upstart " who thought to get on good terms by addressing a villager in the old style was roundly rebuked with the retort, " Don't thee thou me. Thee thou them as thou's thee!"

SATURDAY—MAY 2.

HAVE you ever visited a Japanese garden? The Lady of the House and I saw one at an exhibition a year or two ago and were very impressed by it.

Later, we heard a gardening expert talking about Japanese gardens and how they compare with our own.

Our gardens, he explained, are usually places of activity. We work strenuously in them to keep them in trim; we play in them; we even eat in them. A Japanese garden, on the other hand, is a place of rest and tranquillity, for quiet walking and meditation and gazing at the pools and waterfalls. Most of the plants grow wild, so there is little to do in the way of cultivation.

Perhaps we sometimes run the risk of working so hard in our gardens that we leave ourselves no time to enjoy them! And even if you haven't got a garden, a park or a corner of the countryside will do just as well. We can all have our own "Japanese garden".

MILTON'S COTTAGE

Three hundred years and more have passed
Since poet, blessed by sight and youth
Conjured with words behind these walls,
Combining harmony with truth.

Did he, perhaps, from this same door
Marvel at summer's wealth of blooms?
Did he recall, in later years,
The benison of friendly rooms?

THE FRIENDSHIP BOOK

SUNDAY—MAY 3.

EVERY good gift and every perfect gift is from above. James 1, 17

MONDAY—MAY 4.

THE late Dr Aggrey, the great African educationalist who worked tirelessly for unity between the races, is famous for his saying that, on a piano, you can play some sort of a tune on the black notes alone, and some sort of a tune on the white notes, but for real music, black and white must be played together. So, he argued, black and white races must learn to live together in harmony.

Perhaps one of his less well-known sayings was that education, "is not just a matter of the 3 R's, but of the 3 H's — Head, Hand and Heart."

We may not all be great scholars, but the moral and spiritual development of which Dr Aggrey spoke is a contribution we all can make to the enrichment of life.

TUESDAY—MAY 5.

"WHY don't you walk on the sunny side?" an acquaintance called to me as I strolled along the shaded side of a street.

I was not expected to answer, merely cross and walk alongside her—which I did.

Her remark set me thinking. Often we tend to neglect "the sunny side of life"—dwelling perhaps too much on its sadder aspects.

Of course it is not always easy to be an optimist when things go wrong, but there is generally a streak of silver somewhere to cheer us up if only we look for it. A sunny attitude can be infectious, too, and help others over rough patches.

THE FRIENDSHIP BOOK

<u>WEDNESDAY—MAY 6.</u>

IN a television interview shortly before her death, the well-known entertainer Joyce Grenfell said, "My mother had what I think is a most remarkable gift—that of making goodness sound attractive."

Of course, goodness *ought* to be attractive, but sometimes the way it is presented to us seems a bit off-putting.

It reminds me of the small girl who is reputed to have prayed, "God, please make the bad people good and the good people nice."

Worth thinking about!

<u>THURSDAY—MAY 7.</u>

I WONDER if you know A.A. Milne's amusing poem, "The Old Sailor"? Shipwrecked, the old man begins to think of all the things he needs—water, clothes, a goat and some chickens, a hut to live in, a line and hooks for fishing, and so on.

He begins with the fish hooks, but as he starts to make them the heat of the sun reminds him that he needs a hat, so he starts to make *that,* but soon gets so warm that he goes in search of a spring to cool himself down. Then he thinks of his need of animals and he is looking for these when he remembers that he needs a boat—which means making a sail, and to make a sail he must have needles, and as he is making these he thinks of his need for a hut . . .

So, he thought of his hut and he thought of his boat
And his hat and his breeks and his chickens and
* goat,*
And the hooks (for his food) and the spring (for his
* thirst),*
But he never could think which he ought to do first.

It does help to get your priorities right!

THE FRIENDSHIP BOOK

A FRIEND told me recently about a country walk he took with a group of other people. At one point the route took them into the heart of a wood and after a while they lost the faint pathway they had been following. One member of the group started to panic slightly and suggested turning back the way they had come, but the leader quietly reassured him and after carefully studying his surroundings led off again until they regained the path.

The member who had panicked thanked the leader, but added that he did not know how he could have remained so calm.

"Well," said the leader, "you see, to me the wood is a *friendly* place."

That thought had made all the difference.

WINDMILLS are few and far between now, but few things seem as romantic when you see one in the country. I was interested to read in a book about windmills how millers could use their sails to denote messages. There were different settings of the sail to mark a celebration or mourning. Sails set like a St George's Cross meant "back soon". In smuggling districts, the millers would sometimes have a secret setting as a warning that the customs men were coming!

On Sundays and holidays, the sails were set in the form of a St Andrew's Cross. That should remind us that our holidays were once "holy days".

This is not said to suggest that we should all be ultra-pious, but part of the value of Sundays and holidays is that they should be *different* days from the rest. It is their difference which gives them their value.

THE FRIENDSHIP BOOK

NOW faith is the substance of things hoped for, the evidence of things not seen.   Hebrews 11, 1

THERE is a lot of truth in these verses sent to me by P. J. Barsby of Attenborough, Nottingham:

Some seek to attain, with muscle and brain
*   To win at a sport or a game,*
While some try the Pools, and follow the rules,
*   With winning a fortune their aim.*

Some get their pleasure seeking lost treasure
*   With sensitive counter and rod.*
Some go to the races — just look at their faces,
*   The excitement of winning's their god.*

Yet some are content, their energy spent
*   In doing what makes life worthwhile.*
They may not win races, but see how their faces
*   Light up with their own winning smile!*

SIR ALEXANDER FLEMING, the Scottish scientist, not only discovered penicillin; he also "discovered" a very novel way of putting into practice the familiar dictum, "Say it with flowers".

He used to plant bulbs in his garden in such a way that when they flowered they spelt out names of some of his friends, and then when the flowers were in bloom he invited those friends to stay with him.

An elaborate way of saying "welcome"? Perhaps. But a very much appreciated one, I am sure.

TRANQUILLITY

THE FRIENDSHIP BOOK

WHAT a lot of "secret ministries" go on in life! I'm thinking of the small acts of kindness, the thoughtful deeds, encouraging remarks, the sympathetic listener. The world is full of secret ministers who receive no honours, sometimes no recognition of any sort, not even thanks. Yet without them, how empty life would be!

There is a touching and delightful story told of Sir Hubert von Herkomer, the painter and sculptor, and his father who had also been a great sculptor in his earlier years. Sir Hubert persuaded his elderly father to come and live with him. His father asked for clay that he might not only occupy his time, but also try to keep up his skill.

Sadly the old man's sight was failing and often at nights he would lay aside his work in acute despair. However, after his father had gone to bed, his son would go and work secretly on the clay. In the morning his father would look at his work of the previous evening and, never knowing the "secret ministry" of the night before, would exclaim with delight, "why, it isn't as bad as I thought! I still have some skill left," and so he would start a new day, with uplifted spirits.

I WONDER if you will be alone today? Most of us have to be at some time or other. Paul Tillich, the philosopher, once said that there were two words in the English language which expressed the idea of being alone: "One is 'loneliness' which expresses the pain of being alone; the other is 'solitude' which expresses the glory of being alone."

I know which I shall choose if I am alone today.

THE FRIENDSHIP BOOK

I LIKE the story of the small boy whose mother asked him if he had thanked his hostess when leaving after a party. "Well, no", he replied. "The girl in front of me did and the lady said, 'Don't mention it', so I thought I'd better not!"

WHEN the Lady of the House and I visited our old friend Mary recently, she was sitting in her chair wearing a very attractive hat decorated with flowers.

Thinking she was just preparing to go out we began to apologise and say we would call again.

"Oh no, do sit down," said Mary. "I'm not going out. It's just that I was feeling depressed for some reason when I got up this morning and I find that when I smarten myself up a bit I feel ever so much better. I'm fine now!"

I am sure Mary had a point, and it set me thinking about hats. Do you remember the slogan the hatmakers had some years ago—"If you want to get ahead, get a hat"? Well, I wouldn't know how much truth there is in that, but I remember an article I read once about how certain famous people seem to be symbolised for us by their hats—there was the late Queen Mary's toque, Monty's beret, Maurice Chevalier's boater, Ghandi's forage cap.

But to come back to Mary—whether it's a smart hat, a pretty scarf or blouse, a new suit, these things can give us a bit of an uplift. If you're feeling a bit down in the dumps today, put on something bright, a flower in your hair even! Remember the words from Dickens's "Martin Chuzzlewit"—"Any man may be in good spirits and good temper when he's well dressed."

SWEET HARVEST

THE FRIENDSHIP BOOK

I CAN do all things through Christ which strengtheneth me.   Philippians 4, 13

I THINK morning glory is one of my favourite flowers and I was interested to read in a gardening book that around the world there are more than 400 species of wild morning glories. What delight they must be bringing to millions of people almost everywhere!

Many a morning, especially if the day ahead has held some problem or difficulty, I have gazed at the fleeting delight of the blues and reds and purples and white of my morning glories, and recalled Susan Coolidge's words,

> Every day is a fresh beginning,
> Every morn is the world made new.

SYDNEY SMITH, the 19th century clergyman, traveller, writer and wit, was describing a winter coach journey which he took under stormy skies along muddy roads, through a particularly desolate part of the Cotswolds. The 25 miles, he said, had seemed like 90.

Then, he writes, "Just at the moment when you are taking a melancholy view of human affairs and hating the postillion and blaming the horses, there bursts upon your view, with all its towers, forests and streams, the deep and shaded Vale of Severn."

That journey of his was just like life. When the going gets rough keep your eye firmly on the next bend of the road . . .

F

THE FRIENDSHIP BOOK

WHAT a blessing a sense of humour is, but to get the most out of it we must learn, as someone once said, "to laugh *with* people, not *at* them."

Perhaps even more important is the ability at times to laugh at ourselves.

I like the comment of the old Negro preacher, "If you could jist sit on the fence and see yourself passing by, you'd die laughing at the sight!"

J. M. ROBERTSON calls this poem "Highway Code". It would certainly do none of us any harm to memorise it!:

The road of Life's a winding road
  That twists and turns its way
Through Joy and Jubilation,
  Disappointment and Dismay.
Many are its signposts
  Scattered here and there,
Some can lead to Happiness,
  Others to Despair.
Whatever paths we may pursue,
  This code can aid all men —
Lend a helping hand to those
  Who stumble now and then;
Turn off the avenue to Gloom,
  And make instead for Smile;
Let Reason walk beside you,
  And guide you all the while.
Look yonder! Though the road may seem
  Uncertain — if we tread
With Hope and Courage in our hearts,
  Contentment lies ahead.

THE FRIENDSHIP BOOK

THE artist lying on the scaffolding high above the ground winced as his arms became cramped again. The spasm passed and once more he set to work painting the figures of mythology on the ceiling of the building at the north end of the Terrace overlooking ruined Rievaulx Abbey, North Yorkshire.

It was the middle of the 18th century and the Italian artist, Burnici, had been commissioned by Thomas Duncombe, the owner of the property and "builder" of the Terrace and its Temples, to decorate the ceiling in Italian style.

Burnici often nearly despaired of ever finishing the work, the task was so exhausting, but at length, after seven years, the ceiling was completed. He paid the price of his endurance, dying soon afterwards.

Nowadays visitors to the Temple admire his work, but do not always realise the courage of the artist who suffered so much physical pain to complete it. If there are sermons in stones, there are sometimes lessons in ceilings!

WHETHER or not we are sports fans, I imagine most of us have heard of the great cricketer, Jack Hobbs. I think one of the finest tributes to him was that of John Arlott, the cricket commentator.

He said that when given " out," Hobbs never showed any rancour, but walked smiling from the wicket, raising his bat in a gesture of congratulation to the bowler.

That, surely, is the way to lose, and it applies not only to cricket but to what we sometimes call " the game of life " itself. A smile in defeat is the quickest way to come to terms with it.

THE FRIENDSHIP BOOK

SUNDAY—MAY 24.

A FAITHFUL friend is the medicine of life; and they that fear the Lord shall find him.

Ecclesiasticus 6, 16

MONDAY—MAY 25.

RECENTLY the Lady of the House visited an old friend of ours who had been laid up for some time after an accident. She was surrounded by books, and looking quite cheerful.

"At least *some* good has come out of my accident," she said brightly. "I would never have had time to read all these wonderful books in the ordinary way. I used to laugh sometimes at a saying of my mother's, but I realise now how true it was — 'If life gives you a lemon, make lemonade out of it!'"

If we really try, we can squeeze some good out of even the bitter things of life.

TUESDAY—MAY 26.

THE first Thomas Beecham (usually called "Old Tom" to distinguish him from his distinguished grandson, the conductor) was known to most of his contemporaries as an eccentric millionaire who had made his fortune manufacturing the famous pills that were advertised as being "worth a guinea a box".

But Beecham had a secret of success which, while it may not make us millionaires, is certainly worth pondering. When he was a humble shepherd-boy in the 1830's, he carved on his crook the words: "If you will, you may succeed in wonderful things. Look up. Try again."

He took those words as his motto and never bowed to any adversity. That surely is a secret worth sharing — and more precious than any pill!

THE FRIENDSHIP BOOK

I HAVE no doubt that, as we plan our holidays, we spend a good deal of time consulting guide books of one kind and another. I think we don't always realise what a long history these have. As long ago as 1770, Thomas West wrote "A Guide to the Lakes" — that is, the Lake District as we know it.

His language is often very quaint by our standards. For instance, he wrote of "sweet retreats and enchanted regions of calm repose," and that here one could find "objects to enlarge the mind by contemplation".

Well, I think we might not express it quite like that nowadays! Yet was not his *idea* absolutely right? We do sometimes tend to rush about too much, even on holiday. I know we say "a change is as good as a rest", and a change of scenery and of people can be of enormous benefit to us, but don't let's forget, too, the importance of having "time to stand and stare", of quietness and contemplation. This is part of the truly re-creative power of a holiday and what can make it different from our normal routine.

I had been doing a bit of home decorating when the postman popped a few letters through the letterbox. Wiping my hands I started to open them. I had to smile when I read these lines sent to me by the poet Margaret Bentley:

> *Do it yourself,*
> *is what they say,*
> *Transform your home with colours gay,*
> *But when I do,*
> *it's plain to see,*
> *The thickest paint is all on me.*

JUST RIGHT

*The gentle sweep of curving thatch
By a master's hand is hard to match.*

THE FRIENDSHIP BOOK

I SUPPOSE we all get up "on the wrong side of the bed" now and again. In her book "Journal Of A Solitude", the poet and novelist Mary Sarton tells how one morning she awoke in what she calls "a bad state". She started to go about her household chores as usual, but couldn't throw off her feeling of gloom and depression. Then, suddenly, as she watered her houseplants, the burden seemed to lift just as inexplicably. "I am sure," she said, "it was because I was quietly fulfilling a simple need, a living one."

I think she had discovered a secret we all can share. For her it was the watering of houseplants, but any quiet, simple, loving task can help us find peace of mind.

SOME years ago, a greatly-loved minister died in the little village where he had spent most of his ministry. Practically the whole community attended his funeral service and many were the tributes paid, not so much to his preaching, but to his loving pastoral care for every family.

It was then that his widow revealed something that no-one else knew. Every Saturday evening, as part of his preparation for the Sunday services, he had gone into his empty church and moved from pew to pew, sitting in the places where his people sat, putting himself in their situation, praying for their particular needs, drawing ever closer to them.

JESUS CHRIST the same yesterday, and today and forever.   Hebrews 13, 8

JUNE

<u>MONDAY—JUNE 1.</u>

IN his book "The Life of the Party", Bennett Cerf, the American humorist, gives an excellent example of the importance of turning the limelight away from ourselves.

He says that most of us, writing a "thank-you" note after a week-end visit to a friend, would probably say, "I had a wonderful time." But, says Cerf, how much better to say, "You are a wonderful hostess!"

Only a little different — yet conveying so much more.

<u>TUESDAY—JUNE 2.</u>

I SUSPECT quite a few fathers will recognise themselves in this poem from Miriam Eker, the Manchester poet:

He'd always had a longing,
Right from the very start,
To have a little baby son,
'Twas deep within his heart!
For then he'd have a splendid pal,
His little boy would grow,
They'd go to football matches,
They would swim and fish and row . . .
But when the nurse came in the room,
With leisured, gentle pace,
And called to him, "You've got a girl!"
His heart began to race.
He saw the bundle in her arms,
He felt a surge of joy,
And looking at his daughter,
He forgot about the boy!

THE FRIENDSHIP BOOK

WEDNESDAY—JUNE 3.

MANY lovers of music will treasure memories of Sir Adrian Boult, the great English conductor. The story I like best is of when, during World War II, he was invited to visit a girls' boarding school in Bedford.

Great precautions were taken to leave room for Sir Adrian's car. Other guests arriving early were asked to park well out of the way.

Eventually the great man arrived. He got off his bicycle, removed his cycle clips, and rang the doorbell . . .

THURSDAY—JUNE 4.

MY young friend Allan, just a few doors away, has become an ornithologist. He was given a bird identification book for his birthday and he saved up and bought a pair of binoculars. Now, every spare moment, he's peering at the bushes and trees.

I found him in the park one morning, his glasses focused on a bird rising from the branches.

"I was hoping it was a kestrel," he said. "Do you think it was?"

"Afraid not," I answered. "A pigeon, I think."

He was a bit downcast, but just then I noticed something.

"Quiet," I whispered. "Look at that bunch of thistles. See the small birds on top of the seed-heads?"

Allan gazed in silence as the lovely little goldfinches sent the thistledown floating away while they picked out the seeds.

Allan will soon learn that there are more pigeons and sparrows than kestrels and eagles. But isn't it lovely, I thought, as I walked on, to see a young boy beginning a hobby that will give him pleasure all his days.

THE FRIENDSHIP BOOK

THE 18th century landscape gardener, Lancelot "Capability" Brown, earned his nickname because of his fondness for saying that a site had great "capabilities" — for improvement, that is. We can still see examples of his work at Longleat, Chatsworth, Blenheim, and many other places.

Of course, like all pioneers, he had his detractors. One critic is alleged to have said to him, "I hope I die before you, Mr Brown."

"Oh," was the reply, "why is that?"

"Because I should like to see heaven before you have improved it."

Truly, you can't please everyone!

THE brown and yellow striped jug was a wedding-gift and the Lady of the House always kept it dutifully in view in our sitting-room although, to be honest, neither of us was particularly fond of it. The giver had long since passed on, and one day my better half tentatively suggested it could be a contribution to the coming church jumble sale. "Though who would want it," she added, "goodness knows."

Some weeks later, as we sat in church, she nudged me sharply. "Look at the flower arrangement," she whispered.

There, on the Communion table, was a mass of tawny and gold chrysanthemums. They exactly matched their container — our rejected jug.

"Francis!" she breathed. "It looks exactly right there. It's as if it's come into its own . . . "

I nodded in agreement, marvelling how an ordinary object could be transformed when it was used to the Glory of God.

THE FRIENDSHIP BOOK

SUNDAY—JUNE 7.

A ND they were all filled with the Holy Ghost, and began to speak with other tongues, as the spirit gave them utterance.   Acts 2, 4

MONDAY—JUNE 8.

H ERE'S a bit of useless information I came upon the other day: "There are thousands of miles of coastline in this country, but if all the car owners wished to sit in their cars facing the sea, only one in five would have a front seat view!"

You don't need to take that very seriously, but I can't help feeling that sometimes we spoil our pleasure in what *is,* by thinking about what *might be.* Certainly I don't intend to let those statistics spoil my pleasure in looking at the sea when I feel like it!

TUESDAY—JUNE 9.

R ECENTLY, a Bible salesman in Egypt wrote to tell me of his experiences and recounted an incident when he offered Bibles to a group of young Moslems. One of them accepted a copy, glanced at it briefly, then threw it on the ground and struck the salesman in the face. The salesman simply picked up the Bible and walked away.

A few days later, he went towards another group, not realising that the man who had hit him was among them. This man now rose to greet the salesman saying, "I'm sorry I struck and insulted you. I did so because I'd heard that your Book taught that if a Christian was struck on one cheek, he would turn the other towards his attacker. I wanted to see if you would act according to this teaching. Now I want the Book in which such teaching is given."

THE FRIENDSHIP BOOK

WEDNESDAY—JUNE 10.

WHEN, towards the end of the 15th century, the explorer Bartholomew Diaz was carried by gales round the southern point of Africa, he called that part of the land, "The Cape of Storms".

The Portuguese monarch who had sent him did not approve of the name. He was thinking of the rich lands of the interior and the promise the country held. "No," he said, "we will call it the Cape of Good Hope instead."

It's the kind of vision we all need.

THURSDAY—JUNE 11.

WE all have a secret dream. Jean Forrest wrote to share hers with me, and I know she won't mind if I let you share it, too:

In my dearest, secret dream
I own a cottage small,
With one or two old apple trees,
And ivy on the wall.

Its old-world garden then is mine,
With flowers wild and free,
Red roses on the lintel
To entice the honey-bee.

A wooden seat where oft I sit
And feel the summer sun,
The birdsong waking me each morn,
To say the day's begun.

Through shady, latticed windows
I watch the sun arise.
There's just a touch of Heaven
In my dreamer's paradise.

LICKED!

Which one's for me and which for you?
I don't remember, so I'll just have two!

THE FRIENDSHIP BOOK

THE late Harry Wheatcroft was known world-wide as a rose grower. As a young man, however, he had an ambition to enter politics, and it was an illness in his teens, after which a doctor recommended that he find an open-air occupation, which led to rose-growing in partnership with his brother. He thought of it merely as temporary.

Some time later, James Maxton, a well-known politician of the time, stayed with Wheatcroft's father, an old friend. Young Harry sought Maxton's advice about entering politics. After a pause, Maxton said, "You stick to rose-growing, son. Your roses will bring far more happiness into the world than politics ever will."

Well, I don't suppose we could manage without politicians, but how grateful we ought to be that Harry Wheatcroft took that particular piece of advice!

THE church of King Charles the Martyr in Tunbridge Wells is built across the boundary line of Sussex and Kent, and it is possible to stand inside the church with one foot in either county.

Soon after they were married, a young couple in the town had a violent quarrel. There seemed no chance of their making it up. Then the bride's mother took them both into the church of St Charles, stood one in Kent and the other in Sussex and joined their hands across the boundary. The young couple looked into each other's eyes and the quarrel was forgotten.

It cannot always be done in so romantic a setting, but how truly the touching of hands can often, without words, bridge a gap of enmity or misunderstanding.

THE FRIENDSHIP BOOK

BE not forgetful to entertain strangers: for thereby some have entertained angels unawares.

Hebrews 13, 2

WHEN that much-loved singer, the late Kathleen Ferrier, visited Los Angeles, the conductor Bruno Walter had hoped to act as host to her in his home there. Unfortunately, he had an engagement in New York at the same time, but although he would be absent, he invited her to stay in his home during her visit.

When he eventually returned home, his servants—an Austrian couple—could talk of nothing except how, after a late evening meal, Kathleen Ferrier would call them into the music room and then sit at the piano and sing and play for them—a rare treat, and one that many people would have paid anything for.

I REMEMBER when, a good number of years ago, the Lady of the House and I first made our acquaintance with Mary, now our good friend, we sat in her parlour. Looking out of the window at the church across the way, I asked her, "And is that the church you go to?"

She looked at me steadily for a moment and then replied, with quiet emphasis, "*Go* to? That's the church I *belong* to!"

What a difference between the two things! And what a lot it means really to *belong* — to a church, to a family, to a club, to a group of friends and perhaps, as Mary does now, to a world-wide prayer circle.

"Belonging" is what life is all about.

THE FRIENDSHIP BOOK

A FEW of us were chatting recently and the conversation turned to the state of the world. There were some rather gloomy speculations from two or three of our number. Then someone else lifted us out of our gloom by reciting a little verse, which afterwards, I asked him to write down for me. Here it is:

> *My grandad, viewing earth's worn clogs,*
> *Said things were going to the dogs;*
> *His grandad in his house of logs,*
> *Said things were going to the dogs;*
> *His grandad in the Flemish bogs*
> *Said things were going to the dogs;*
> *His grandad in his old skin togs,*
> *Said things were going to the dogs;*
> *There's one thing that I have to state—*
> *The dogs have had a good long wait!*

A SMALL boy heard someone use the expression "human beings" and asked what it meant.

"It means all of us," he was told. "Father, mother, brother, sister, our neighbours. Everyone we know is a human being."

"But, all the people we don't know — are they human beings, too?" he asked.

How easy it is sometimes to think only of those within our immediate circle! It might not be a bad idea as we read our newspapers today or watch the news on television, in which there will be much about so many people we do not know, just to try and think of a few of them at least, not just as items of news, but as human beings, as persons deserving our concern.

THE FRIENDSHIP BOOK

O UR new young neighbour only came in to borrow some vanilla for the birthday cake she was making. However, the Lady of the House made a pot of tea and together they spent a good 20 minutes round the kitchen table, poring over various recipe books.

When we were on our own again I remarked on how well the two of them had got on. There had been an instant rapport between them.

The Lady of the House, who is also my very wisest sage, then explained. "A new neighbour," she said, "becomes a friend as soon as she steps over the doorstep."

" A PRON STRINGS" is the title of this lovely poem by that fine poet, Fay Inchfawn:

From holy hopes and wistful fears,
From age-long dreams, from listening ears,
From memories of sweet good-nights,
From trivial every-day delights,
From little loving ministries,
Warm hands and supplicating knees,
Yes, out of just such common things
God made a mother's apron strings!

So frail they seem, and yet their hold
Is stronger far than chains of gold.
They have drawn men from No Man's Land
Back to their own familiar strand.
The mariner in wintry blast,
Just as redemption point was past,
Has caught at them, and found that wings
Grew from his mother's apron strings!

G

THE FRIENDSHIP BOOK

SUNDAY—JUNE 21.

HAVE we not all one father? Hath not one God created us?

Malachi 2, 10

MONDAY—JUNE 22.

MANY of us put a vase of flowers or a plant in our window, but a friend who has just returned from a holiday in Holland says he has never seen so many window decorations in his life. Often, every windowsill in the house is packed tight with plants; and in not only houses, but shops, offices and factories. Even when he took a canal cruise, the captain's bridge was similarly decorated with beautiful plants.

We talk about having a "good" holiday, but my friend describes his as the most "cheerful" holiday he has ever had. What happiness we can spread when we try to bring a bit of beauty into everyday life!

TUESDAY—JUNE 23.

IN one of his books, Dr Stanley Jones writes about Dr George Carver, the American negro who was well-known as a Christian leader and as an agricultural scientist. He was subject to much prejudice, misunderstanding and opposition—including rejection as a student by a university which had accepted him before realising that he was a negro.

But all this Dr Carver suffered bravely and patiently in the strength of his Christian faith. Dr Jones makes a remark about him which I shall never forget: "He not only had the peace which passeth all understanding, but the peace which passeth all misunderstanding."

That really *is* peace of heart.

THE FRIENDSHIP BOOK

THE Lady of the House came in bursting with excitement. "Do you know what I saw at the art exhibition?" she asked and didn't wait for an answer. "The most beautiful church embroidery. The colours were lovely. It's a fall to hang over the pulpit, and wall hangings as well. And do you know who did them?"

"Somebody I know?" I asked.

"Of course! Little Mrs Robinson. I never knew she had such a gift. I said that to her and she said she hadn't known it either."

I waited for the Lady of the House to explain.

"Well, you know she has a handicapped daughter to look after and she hardly ever gets out of the house. The doctor told her if she didn't find an outside interest she would be heading for a breakdown. She didn't know what to do, but she saw some embroidery classes advertised and she thought she would give them a try."

"And found she had a natural gift?"

"Yes, and now she's done these beautiful things. And to think that if her doctor hadn't insisted that she get out of the house just for two or three hours a week she would never have known she had this gift. Isn't it strange how things work out, Francis?"

I agreed.

YOUNG Billy from next door caught me out with another of his jokes one sunny day recently.

"Mr Gay," he asked seriously, "do you know why the days are longer in Summer than in Winter?"

I hesitated just that second too long, and as he ran off down the street he called over his shoulder, "They expand with the heat!"

SMOOTH SAILING

Not for me the rolling sea
    And a stinging, salty breeze,
But the gentler draught of river craft
    And the dappled shade of trees,
Song bird cries, butterflies
    And heavy-laden bees.

THE FRIENDSHIP BOOK

WHEN the townsfolk of Strasbourg were digging in the ruins of their church, bombed during the course of the Last War, they found their statue of Christ lying buried deep in the rubble. Thankfully it was undamaged, except for the hands, which had been broken off and smashed.

A famous sculptor offered to replace the hands without charge as his own personal contribution to the rebuilding of the church, but the congregation refused.

Today, visitors to that German church can see the statue — still without hands. "It reminds us," the local people say, "that Christ has no hands but ours to do His work."

WHICH is the very worst sin of all? The one which Rudyard Kipling put high on his list rather surprised me when I came across this remark in his famous novel "Kim", the story of the orphaned white boy who grew up as a lively, enterprising Indian. It was a remark made by the English officer who is training Kim: "There is no sin so great as ignorance. Remember this."

I think I see what he meant. To be unwilling to learn about the wonderful world in which we live, to fail to take an interest in other people and life in general — well, this is sin indeed, because it is the sin of pride and self-sufficiency. Learning something new each day can help us to grow in grace.

JUDGE not according to the appearance, but judge righteous judgment.   John 7, 24

THE FRIENDSHIP BOOK

MONDAY—JUNE 29.

I HAD to smile at the description of a certain Italian hotel. Its house brochure read as follows:

"This hotel is renowned for its peace and tranquillity. In fact, crowds from all over the world flock here to enjoy its solitude."

TUESDAY—JUNE 30.

ONE of the most generous men of last century was the writer the Rev. Charles Kingsley — not always with money for he was frequently short himself, but with warm-hearted praise and encouragement to his family, friends, students and even casual acquaintances.

He sincerely believed that his younger brother, Henry, was a greater novelist than himself, and on Henry's return from Australia with the manuscript of a book he had written there, "Geoffrey Hamlyn", Charles did everything possible to help get it published. He also found other writing outlets for Henry.

In spite of his work as a clergyman, writer and lecturer, Charles found time to keep up a correspondence with people all over the world. And he always had time to pay tribute to the good work done by others. When his friend Charles Mansfield died. Charles Kingsley wrote: "He was always thinking how to please others in the most trivial matters; not to make them think well of him (which breeds only affection), but just to make them comfortable; and that is why he left a trail of light wherever he went."

It's a description which aptly fits Kingsley himself. He, too, left "a trail of light" which still shines today from the stories and poems he bequeathed to the world.

JULY

WEDNESDAY—JULY 1.

WHEN Albert Schweitzer arrived at a party given in his honour, the butler turned him away from the front door and sent him round to the servants' entrance. This elderly man with unkempt hair and a shabby suit could not possibly be the world-famous musician, physician, and philosopher he had been told to look out for.

The surprising thing was not the butler's mistake, but the doctor's reaction. With a mixture of humour and humility, Schweitzer quietly obeyed, and so arrived at his own party via the back door.

THURSDAY—JULY 2.

I THINK people often quote those inspiring words, "God's in His heaven, all's right with the world", without knowing their source. In fact, they come from the well-known poem by Robert Browning, "Pippa Passes".

Pippa was a silk weaver in Asolo, Italy, who was allowed only one day's holiday in the whole year. Waking on the morning of her holiday she wasted no time lamenting that she has just the one day, but set out to enjoy every moment of it:

O Day, if I squander a wavelet of thee,
A mite of thy twelve hours' treasure
The least of thy gazes or glances . . .
One of thy choices or one of thy chances . . .
My Day, if I squander such labour or leisure
Then shame fall on Asolo, mischief on me.

A good thought with which to start *any* day, not just a holiday!

THE FRIENDSHIP BOOK

A READER who is a lover of sea stories and a great fan of Joseph Conrad, sent me a quotation from his favourite author and asks, "What do you think of this, when we have to face what we call 'the storms of life'? It is from "Typhoon" and gives advice on how to deal with such a crisis: 'Always *facing* it, Captain McWhirr. That's the way to get through.'"

I imagine many of us have found that to be true.

SOME time ago, on holiday in Lincolnshire, the Lady of the House and I stood admiring the famous Boston Stump — the great church tower that stretches upward for 275 feet.

An old man approached us. "Wonderful, isn't it?" he said. We agreed that it was, and then he continued, "I will tell you something else wonderful, too. There are seven doors in the church to represent the seven days of the week; 12 pillars in the nave for the 12 months; 24 steps to the library for the hours of the day; 52 windows for the weeks of the year; 60 steps to the chancel roof for the seconds in a minute; 365 steps to the top of the tower for the days in the year."

Then, as he moved away, he said, "You see, we can't get away from time in Boston!"

Well, nor can any of us! Time is a gift, a trust, an opportunity. The nursery verses of Jane Taylor, who wrote "Twinkle, Twinkle, Little Star", may seem a bit old fashioned nowadays, but there is still a lot of wisdom in the words,

> *How pleasant it is at the end of the day*
> *No follies to have to repent,*
> *But reflect on the past and be able to say*
> *That my time has been properly spent.*

THE FRIENDSHIP BOOK

HE shall feed his flock like a shepherd: he shall gather the lambs with his arm and carry them in his bosom.　　　　　　　　　　　　　Isaiah 40, 11

MONDAY—JULY 6.

LITTLE Davie McPhail loved to fly his kite. There is nothing very unusual about that — thousands of boys must share the same pleasure. The difference is that Davie was blind.

People would sometimes express surprise that he should enjoy flying a kite when he couldn't see it. His answer was always the same: "No, I can't see it, but I like to feel its pull."

We sometimes say, "Seeing is believing", yet, when you come to think about it there are lots of things in life that we can't *see*, but we *feel* their influence all the same.

TUESDAY—JULY 7.

DR DONALD COGGAN, the well loved Archbishop of Canterbury, once described a visit to a small country church in the following way: " The priest was not a remarkable man as the world might judge, and the music was not up to the standard of Canterbury Cathedral, yet I felt on the edge of eternity."

I have my own favourite little church. It is always beautiful with flowers and it is never closed. Near the old Saxon door there is this printed welcome: " You are always welcome here, whether you have faith or not. You can find forgiveness here, strength for the present, and hope for the future—and then go away with courage and with peace ".

And so I do.

H

THE FRIENDSHIP BOOK

I LIKE this little story about William Wilberforce who worked so hard to abolish slavery.

" O Massa Wilbyfoss," exclaimed a grateful negro girl, " bless you, sah! You hab white skin, but you hab black heart."

I am sure there wasn't the slightest risk of that tribute being misinterpreted.

IT'S wonderful what we come across when we turn out an old drawer. A Manchester lady was doing just this when she discovered these verses written, she thinks, at least 60 years ago. For those who don't know Lancashire dialect she adds that "gradely" is a word applied to something very good:

> Give us, Lord, a bit o' sun,
> A bit o' work and a bit o' fun;
> Give us all, in the struggle and splutter,
> Our daily bread and a bit o' butter.
>
> Give us our health our keep to make,
> And a bit to spare for poor folks' sake;
> Give us sense, for we're some of us duffers,
> An' a heart to feel for all that suffers.
>
> Give us, too, a bit o' a song,
> An' a tale an' a book to help us along;
> An' give us our share o' sorrow's lesson
> That we may prove how grief's a blessin'.
>
> Give us, Lord, a chance to be
> Our gradely best, brave wise and free,
> Our gradely best for oursels and others
> Till all men learn to live as brothers.

THE FRIENDSHIP BOOK

THE late Sir Billy Butlin, the "Holiday Camp King" as he has been called, tells in his autobiography how he had always been fond of gardens, but, of course, when he was a travelling showman in his early days, living in a caravan, he couldn't have one.

When he started his holiday camps he determined that gardens should have a prominent place in them. He started at Skegness where he planted rose trees. One evening, when he was walking round the camp, he met an old lady coming out of her chalet carrying a glass of water which she carefully poured round the roots of one of the rose bushes.

Seeing Billy Butlin's curious look, she explained, "I pretend it's my own tree for the week of my holiday!"

If we have a garden, a window box, even a single plant, let us be grateful for it, care for it, and rejoice that it is our own!

THE Lady of the House chuckled as she was reading one of her magazines. I looked up questioningly, and she said, "This is true, Francis, isn't it? 'Housework is something that nobody notices until you don't do it'."

I had to admit it *is* true. But it is true of other things, too, isn't it? There are so many things we take for granted and really notice only when they stop, or are disrupted in some way. It is when a bus is late, or the newspaper boy forgets to deliver the paper, or there is a power cut, that we begin to realise how full life is of benefits that we never really notice or appreciate — until they stop!

THE FRIENDSHIP BOOK

A ND the glory of the Lord shall be revealed, and all flesh shall see it together: for the mouth of the Lord hath spoken it.   Isaiah 40, 5

A FRIEND sent me this item from his church magazine. At the top of the page was a small blank square, outlined in black, followed by these instructions:

Breathe on this square, then,

1. If it turns red, see your bank manager.
2. If it turns blue, see your solicitor.
3. If it turns green, see your doctor.
4. If it turns yellow, see your optician.
5. If it does not change colour, you are perfectly healthy and there is no reason for you not to be in church next Sunday!

S OME of the old autograph albums, so popular a generation or two back, can be rich sources of inspirational thoughts. Here is one I came across recently, as I browsed through the pages of a friend's book:

Ships sail East and ships sail West
Wherever the winds may blow:
For it's the set of the sails
And not the gales
That determines the way we go.

It's definitely a good thought for those occasions when we tend to blame our circumstances and not ourselves!

THE FRIENDSHIP BOOK

THE first Henry Ford had a now-famous saying attributed to him, "History is bunk!" What a lot of people there are who, in the same way, dismiss things which could probably give a good deal of happiness if only they would try them. "It bores me to be in the country," they say, or "Art galleries leave me cold."

I remember the remark of a man who had never been interested in music, yet through the encouragement of his wife, came to appreciate it greatly. He said, "Classical music isn't as bad as it sounds!"

Don't let's be like the Englishman on holiday in Scotland who declined haggis, saying, "I don't like it; I've never tasted it."

There's so much we can learn to appreciate if only we make the effort. Let's make a start today.

BILL loves working in wood, and I often admire the beautiful objects he makes.

One day I called on him, and all around his workshop were examples of his craft — a nest of tables, bowls, a chess board, a Saxony spinning wheel and chair of authentic design. I asked him where the wood had come from and Bill smiled. "Do you remember those old desks and chairs that the school threw out last year?"

I was amazed when he told me that everything there had been made from material discarded as useless and unwanted.

His craftsman's eye had seen the potential in what others considered be "rubbish". All that was required was the touch of a master's hand.

HUMBLING

How puny the attempts of man
To set the world to rights,
When viewed beside a masterpiece
Of Nature's wondrous sights.
Remember with humility
How small is our ability.

THE FRIENDSHIP BOOK

THERE is a story — not to be believed, of course — concerning an absent-minded schoolmaster who took some children on a trip and brought home more pupils than he had started with!

Yet, as somebody once said, "Life always gives to us more than we give to it." We can gain from every experience, good or bad, if we determine to do so. Let us put what we can into today — in service, hope, and faith — and we shall find that tonight we will have more than we set out with.

DURING the American War of Independence, a group of soldiers under the direction of a corporal was trying to heave a beam into position with ropes. Time and time again, when success was almost in sight, the beam slipped because the men just hadn't quite the strength needed. And all the while, the corporal stood by shouting, "Heave! Heave!"

A man in civilian clothes paused for a moment to watch. Then he said quietly to the corporal, "Don't you think if you lent a hand the men might manage the job?"

"I?" said the corporal, on his dignity. "But I am a corporal!" Without a word, the stranger took off his coat and joined the men on the ropes. With the next haul the task was completed.

The helper put on his coat, saying, "Well, we managed that together, gentlemen," then turning to the corporal added quietly, "If you have this sort of difficulty again, just send for the Commander-in-Chief. I shall always be glad to help."

It was then that the self-important little corporal realised the helper was George Washington!

THE FRIENDSHIP BOOK

A ND it shall come to pass in the last days that the mountain of the Lord's house shall be established in the top of the mountains, and shall be exalted above the hills.   Isaiah 2, 2

Y EARS ago, a member of the United States Congress, Mr Solly Bloom, used to carry in his pocket a handful of shiny new one cent coins. From time to time, he would place one on the pavement. Sometimes he would stop a little way off and watch a stranger pick up the money.

He said that regardless of whether the person looked poor or affluent, the coin always brought a smile to the face of the discoverer. As Solly himself said, "It doesn't take much to make people smile."

How true. Let's try it today — not by copying Solly Bloom's method, but by inventing one of our own.

M Y tree-climbing days were over many years ago and I expect yours were, too. Even so, we can all appreciate the wisdom behind this little saying seen on a poster in the porch of a little church in Essex:

"He who would climb a tree must grasp the branches—not the blossom."

The blossoms are the pleasures of this life — and, of course, we all deserve our share of these. But the branches are what support us and help us on our way. They are our faith, our code of living and our trust in the Almighty. If these are strong, we have nothing to fear.

THE FRIENDSHIP BOOK

WEDNESDAY—JULY 22.

WE all like to daydream, don't we? Margaret Bentley of Bradford found herself doing it one day and afterwards she wrote this poem:

This evening will see me the talk of the town,
I'll be wearing a fabulous, shimmering gown.
My hairstyle will be absolutely exotic,
The effect on the men will be simply chaotic.
My escort will be someone quite debonair,
Not only a catch — he's a real millionaire.

I'm up to my elbows in soapsuds and wishes,
Better come down to earth — and this sink
full of dishes!

THURSDAY—JULY 23.

I AM not much of a theologian, but I must admit I was intrigued when in the "Prayer Handbook of the Council for World Mission" I came across the term "coconut theology"!

It is a phrase used among the churches of the Solomon Islands in the Pacific and sprang from the way in which the coconut palm has spread from one island to another through ocean currents carrying the seeds from shore to shore.

The churches in these islands had often felt isolated, and they saw in this a parable of the way in which their faith had to be shared and carried from one place to another.

This is true not simply of religion, but of all the good and great and glad things of our lives. It's a matter of giving and receiving and sharing and togetherness. Here's a "theology" we can all understand and put into practice in everyday situations.

THE FRIENDSHIP BOOK

I AM always intrigued by unusual place-names. Maybe I would never have come across Stanford-in-the-Vale-cum-Goosey in Berkshire if it had not been at one time the home of the scholar and hymn-writer, Christopher Wordsworth, nephew of the famous Lakeland poet.

One of his best-known hymns begins:

> *O Lord of heaven and earth and sea,*
> *To Thee all praise and glory be;*
> *How shall we show our love to Thee,*
> *Giver of all?*

Local tradition says that Christopher, when he was rector of the village, was disturbed at the smallness of the church collections and wrote the hymn to stimulate the generosity of the congregation. He included the hymn in the service every few weeks, and it's said that it worked!

I don't know if that story is true, but I do know that the beauty of the world should always stir us to gratitude and gladness.

OUR neighbour, Billy, was waiting for me at the garden gate when I went out the other day.

"Would you like to hear my imitation of bagpipes in the distance, Mr Gay?"

What could I say but, "Yes"!

So Billy cupped his hands, blew into them, puffing out his cheeks till they were red, but no sound came. At last he stopped and said, "I'm sorry, Mr Gay—they're too far away for you to hear!"

Then he ran off, as well he might, before I had time to reply.

THE FRIENDSHIP BOOK

A FOOL uttereth all his mind: but a wise man keepeth it in till afterwards.   Proverbs 29, 11

WHEN the writers, Wilfred and Alice Meynell, first met the poet Francis Thompson he was down and out, verging on despair. They opened their home to him and treated him as a member of the family.

Sometimes Thompson would disappear for days at a time, but he always felt drawn back to them, and however black his mood, he had only to come into Wilfred Meynell's presence to be lifted up in spirit and hope.

We shall probably never find ourselves in the dramatic situation of the Meynells, but there is always someone near us in need of sympathy and comfort.

ONE of the annual events on television to which the Lady of the House and I look forward is the Young Musician of the Year Competition.

Apart from the music itself, we enjoy the comments of these young people on the piece they have chosen and upon their own peformance. Just after one young lady had played her piece, she was asked, "Did you enjoy playing that?" She hesitated for a moment and then said, "No, not really."

"Why, what was wrong?" asked the interviewer.

"Well, I would rather make music with other people than alone," she replied.

Of course, there *are* solitary pleasures we can enjoy, but how much of life's real enjoyment comes from doing things together!

THE FRIENDSHIP BOOK

A GOOD example of someone not saying quite what he meant was given to me by a friend who had been to a special service culminating with the dedication of an item of church furniture. The minister was anxious that the congregation should remain standing while the dedication took place, so he announced, " We shall rise and sing hymn 247, and we shall continue rising during the act of dedication "!

A BUSINESSMAN who suffered from insomnia was asking a friend how he managed to sleep so soundly every night. "Do you count sheep?" he asked.

"No," came the reply. "I just talk to the Shepherd."

TODAY is the feast day of Ignatius of Loyola, founder of the Society of Jesus in the 16th century. His conversion is said to have come about when, as a young soldier, he spent a long period convalescing from wounds received in battle. He spent the time reading widely about the life of Jesus and the saints.

On this day we might well remember and use his great prayer:

Teach us, good Lord,
To serve Thee as Thou deservest;
To give and not to count the cost;
To fight and not to heed the wounds;
To toil and not to seek for rest;
To labour and not to ask for any reward
Save that of knowing that we do Thy will.

FISHING

Into the river with nets we wade;
Such exciting discoveries can be made.

AUGUST

SATURDAY—AUGUST 1.

WE all enjoy times of solitude. J. M. Robertson has written a thoughtful poem on the subject:

Oft in quiet solitude,
I think, in retrospective mood,
Of all the days and years gone by,
Of memories that will not die.

I think of times so long ago,
Acquaintances I used to know,
And how they used to stop and share
A little joy, a little care.

I think of moments in the past
When happiness just had to last.
Its light with bright endeavour shone,
As if to warn — dull care, begone!

I think of many golden days,
All special in so many ways.
Good times were had by one and all;
Bad times? Nothing to recall.

Oft in lonely solitude,
I think in recollective mood,
Reviving an old cavalcade
Of memories that cannot fade.

SUNDAY—AUGUST 2.

AND Jesus said unto them, I am the bread of life: he that cometh to me shall never hunger, and he that believeth on me shall never thirst.   John 6, 35

THE FRIENDSHIP BOOK

MONDAY—AUGUST 3.

IN recent years, there has been a revival on August 1st (or the Sunday nearest to it) of the ancient Lammas Day custom of bringing the first fruits of the corn, or a loaf baked from it (hence, Loaf Mass, from Anglo-Saxon *hlafmaesse*) into church.

A little later in the year, of course, come the full Harvest Thanksgiving services when "all is safely gathered in".

I like the idea of the earlier celebration, not so much of achievement, but of promise and of hope and of confidence in the future. How much we need those qualities, not only in the realm of Nature, but in the whole of life.

TUESDAY—AUGUST 4.

YEARS ago, when King George VI visited a town in Northern England, a boy in the crowd was heard to say, in some disappointment, "Why, he's nobbut a fellow!" Quite what he expected the king to be, I do not know.

Yet, in a sense, George VI was just a man — a very humble man. The story is told that the night before the Coronation, the Dean of Westminster received a telephone message from him saying, "I want to come to the Abbey tonight." "Certainly, sir," said the Dean. "I will be there to receive you." "No, don't do that," George replied. "Just see that the postern door is left open. I wish to come into the Abbey and I wish to be alone."

And there he kept his solitary vigil in the spot where, the following day, amid all the pomp of the Coronation, huge crowds would attend. Humanity and humility — these indeed were the marks of a great kingship.

THE FRIENDSHIP BOOK

WHEN the Lady of the House and I were window-shopping the other day, we saw in a second-hand bookshop a card with these words written on it:

> *The bookshop has a thousand books,*
> *All colours, hues and tinges,*
> *And every cover is a door*
> *That turns on magic hinges.*

I am sure that the man who kept that shop was not just a bookseller; he was a booklover. I must try to capture something of that magic when I next open a book . . .

SOME years ago, a church, planning to celebrate its centenary, was preparing a handbook for the occasion. The original building had been destroyed by fire many years before and no photographs or drawings survived.

Wishing to paint a picture of it for the handbook, an artist asked the handful of people who remembered the building if they would try to draw what they recalled. All of them disclaimed any skill as artists, but they promised to have a go.

From their very varied attempts, the painter compiled a picture of what he thought the building had looked like. When the others saw it, they all said it was exactly as they remembered, even though their own individual attempts had been very far from perfect.

What a lot of things there are which we can't do individually, but which, when we work together, can be achieved beyond our dreams.

UNFORGETTABLE
Hill and stream together capture
A golden day of careless rapture.

THE FRIENDSHIP BOOK

THERE is an old saying, "All work and no play makes Jack a dull boy." That puts me in mind of a 17th century Dean of St. Paul's, Dr Nowel.

He believed in the Biblical custom of tithing, but gave to the idea what must have been considered by many to be a rather eccentric twist. He not only donated a tenth of his income to religious and charitable causes, but also insisted on giving a tenth of his time to leisure!

His epitaph bears witness to his wisdom:

He died 13th February 1601, aged 95 years, 44 of which he had been Dean of St. Paul's Cathedral. His age had neither impaired his hearing, nor dimmed his eyes nor weakened his memory, nor made any of the faculties of his mind weak or useless.

As someone said of him, "Recreation and religion kept him young." An arguable thought? Maybe, but one worth pondering.

DAME EVA TURNER, the singer, has been called "The Grand Duchess of Opera". When she was 92 she appeared on the television programme, "This Is Your Life".

One of the guests was the Welsh singer, Sir Geraint Evans, who told how he had visited Dame Eva when she was in hospital for a serious eye operation which looked as if it might put an end to her career as she would be unable to read music. He found her undaunted. Cheerfully she told him, "If this operation is not successful, I shall still be able to *hear* great singing."

THE FRIENDSHIP BOOK

SUNDAY—AUGUST 9.

EVEN a child is known by his doings, whether his work be pure, and whether it be right.

Proverbs 20, 11

MONDAY—AUGUST 10.

I HAVE heard many different definitions of an optimist, but a friend came up with one that was new to me: " An optimist is someone who takes the cold water thrown upon an idea, heats it with enthusiasm and then uses the steam to push ahead."

TUESDAY—AUGUST 11.

I LOVE walking round old Tom Turner's garden with him, because not only can he tell me the names (English *and* Latin!) of all the flowers, but he also has an interesting story about most of them.

The other day, for example, he pointed out the forget-me-nots. "Look at those curved flower-bearing stems, Francis," he said. "Like scorpions' tails, aren't they? You know, that's the reason people once thought the plant could heal the sting of scorpions."

We walked a little farther. "Pansies always remind me of Ophelia's words, 'There is pansies, that's for thoughts'. I think the name is probably derived from the French *pensée,* a thought."

He glanced over the wall into the lane beyond where some purple loosestrife was growing. "That's an interesting name, too, Francis," he said. "People used to say if you took some of that home, it would prevent strife in the family."

What truth there is in Tom's stories I wouldn't know, but I *do* know that when I look at many of the flowers in my own garden, their names give an extra bonus to their beauty.

IT'S MAGIC

Don't believe Dad when he says it's a pond.
Over there, through the arch, is the Land of Beyond!

THE FRIENDSHIP BOOK

IN a discussion group at church we were talking about prayer when one of our older members, Jamie Ferguson, rather surprised, then intrigued, and finally inspired me as he explained how, for part of his prayers, he uses a map of the world.

On a stormy night, he will look at the North Sea and think of the fishermen in their perilous work. If a trouble-spot of the world has been mentioned in the news, he will pin-point that place in his prayers. If he has friends abroad on holiday, he follows them in thought. In a week he has probably gone round the world!

I think a number of us went away from that meeting determined to make some prayer journeys.

A FRIEND of ours has a collection of birthday cards going back over 50 years. Browsing through some of them, I came across these words which, old-fashioned as they may appear, seem to me much more inspiring than some modern verses I've read:

> Count your garden by the flowers,
> Never by the leaves that fall;
> Count your days by golden hours,
> Don't remember clouds at all.
>
> Count your nights by stars, not shadows,
> Count your life by smiles not tears;
> And with joy, upon your birthday,
> Count your age by friends not years.

We don't need to wait for our birthday to do that bit of counting. We can do it today!

THE FRIENDSHIP BOOK

WHEN the Lady of the House and I visit old churches, I think one of our chief delights is in some of the gloriously-coloured stained glass windows especially when the sun shines through, casting a many-coloured pattern on the floor.

Some of the windows depict Biblical scenes or saints. Others are modern, some simply in the form of decorative patterns.

I read of a church where all the windows except one are stained glass. The exception is plain glass through which you can see the trees in the churchyard, the fields and hills beyond, and the sky overhead.

Below the window, carved in the stonework, are words from the Psalms: "The heavens declare the glory of God and the firmament showeth his handiwork."

This must be one of the most beautiful windows of them all.

IN the organ-loft of Whitfields Tabernacle in London, destroyed by enemy action in March 1945, was this inscription:

Make a large place in your life for music and it will bring you a priceless reward.

In the hour of rest, music will lift up your spirit and give refreshment to every faculty of your being.

In the hour of work, you will rejoice in the strength and energy which music has given you.

In the hour of prayer, music will quicken the aspirations of your soul.

In the hour of fellowship, music will blend your spirit with others in unity and understanding.

THE FRIENDSHIP BOOK

FOR wisdom is better than rubies; and all the things that may be desired are not to be compared to it.   Proverbs 8, 11

YEHUDI MENUHIN, the world-famous violinist, clearly has a very great musical gift; but he has something else, too, which contributes to his astonishing success — he has a great capacity for giving.

Some years ago at a summer concert in the Lewishohn Stadium in New York, Menuhin remained playing encores long after the orchestra had left and the lights had been turned out. Under the stars he poured out his soul in music which, because it meant so much to him, meant much to those who heard it, too.

His joy is in giving, in sharing his great gift with others.

I was interested recently to hear in a church service the members of a Boys' Brigade company singing the old hymn, not often heard nowadays, "Will your anchor hold in the storms of life?" An anchor, of course, forms part of the B.B. badge.

It reminded me that the symbolism of the anchor goes a long, long way back in history. The ancient Greek philosopher and mathematician Pythagoras, wrote: "Wealth is a weak anchor; fame is still weaker. What then are the anchors which are strong? Wisdom, great-heartedness, courage — these are the anchors which no storm can shake."

That's still true, after all these centuries.

STABLE TALK

I've only been gone a few minutes,
I said I'd come back without fail;
I left you my kitten for company,
How COULD you have stood on her tail?

THE FRIENDSHIP BOOK

T HE Lady of the House came in chuckling the other day. She had just met a couple who had recently returned from a farmhouse holiday in Somerset.

It seems that Robert invariably asks for porridge for breakfast, no matter where he is, and when his wife noticed that he was the only person in the dining room being served porridge, she said to the farmer's wife, "I'm so sorry if you had to make the porridge specially for my husband."

"That's all right, dear," came the reply. "We had to make it for the pigs anyway."

D R ALBERT SCHWEITZER was once rehearsing a Bach Prelude on the organ in Ulm Cathedral. He had with him a friend, and Schweitzer asked him to go into the body of the church and then call up each time he tried different stops to tell him how it sounded far below.

"I love to listen," said the friend, "but I really know nothing at all about music. I can't play a note."

"That's why I want your opinion," said Schweitzer. "You will be able to tell me the effect on ordinary listeners without being distracted by technicalities of all kinds."

Of course, there is a place for technicalities in music as in much else, but very often, too, there is enjoyment to be had in things we really don't understand. For us ordinary folk, appreciation is often quite as important as understanding. None of us needs to miss out on the enjoyment that can be found in music, art, literature, the world of Nature and much else, just because our technical knowledge is incomplete.

THE FRIENDSHIP BOOK

OLDER readers will remember the popular war-time song containing the words:

> . . .when you turned and smiled at me
> A nightingale sang in Berkeley Square.

Well, that's nonsense, of course: there are no nightingales in London's Berkeley Square! But the Australian preacher, Dr F. W. Boreham, once made a very apt comment about the lyrics. He claimed that the words were not as foolish as they sounded. Because of the smile, the air had *seemed* full of bird-song. "It's not the nightingales which bring the smile; it is the smile that brings the nightingales," he said.

Does your smile bring out the nightingales?

IN the Thirties, one of the leading lights in Oxford's musical circles was Miss Margaret Deneke, who was very active in the Women's Institute Movement as well as the social and cultural life of the city.

I love the story they still tell of her versatility — how once when speaking at a Women's Institute meeting, she divided her talk into two parts. The first was a mini-lecture on, "Brahms — the man and the composer"; the second was a practical demonstration on how to skin a rabbit!

Incongruous? Not to Margaret Deneke or her audience. What a mistake it is to think that if people are artistic, they are necessarily impractical, and vice-versa!

How much richer we should all be if we paid attention to both sides of life.

THE FRIENDSHIP BOOK

<u>SUNDAY—AUGUST 23.</u>

FEAR God, and keep his commandments: for this is the whole duty of man.　　Ecclesiastes 12, 13

<u>MONDAY—AUGUST 24.</u>

I AGREE with every word of this little poem by Miriam Eker:

> *Try and talk to people,*
> *And maybe you will find*
> *That underneath their quiet reserve*
> *They're really very kind.*
> *Remember, folks are often shy,*
> *And sometimes not so sure,*
> *But very ready to respond,*
> *If you make an overture.*
> *There really is no telling*
> *Where such a talk can end —*
> *You may be quite surprised to find*
> *That you have made a friend!*

<u>TUESDAY—AUGUST 25.</u>

IT was the Sunday School anniversary and our preacher chose a theme not unusual for such occasions — "Child-likeness" (not *"childishness"*, he warned us!) But he used a quotation which was new to me and set me thinking. He reported that the eminent novelist, Arnold Bennett, once said, "The only way to write a great book is to write it through the eyes of a child who sees things for the first time."

"The first time" — how important that is. We get so *accustomed* to things. They lose their wonder for us. We've seen it, done it, heard it all before . . .

Today I am going to try and look at some things as though I was seeing them for the very first time.

SHARING

A bright and cheerful garden
Is a pleasant thing to tend,
And its beauty brings enjoyment
Shared with every passing friend.

THE FRIENDSHIP BOOK

WEDNESDAY—AUGUST 26.

THE following good advice was given by an elderly parson to a newly-married couple:

" I want to give you this advice, my children—don't *try* to be happy. Happiness is a shy nymph, and if you chase her you will never catch her. Just go quietly on, and do your duty, and she will come to you." Sound advice for us all.

THURSDAY—AUGUST 27.

RECENTLY I came across an unusual and fascinating book called "Street Flowers" by Richard Mabey. The author admits that town and city streets seem unlikely places to discover wild flowers. Yet he points out that there are cracks between the paving stones and in old walls, rubble by building sites, dirt washed into the gutters, strips of land at the edges of factories and railway lines. In these, and many similar places, he has discovered coltsfoot, red clover, shepherd's purse, golden rod, burdock, and many other wild flowers.

It will certainly make me keep my eyes open for similar discoveries, and act as a reminder that, in other ways, too, if we look for it, we can find beauty in unexpected places.

FRIDAY—AUGUST 28.

MOTHER TERESA of Calcutta is known, respected and loved for her compassion for the poor, and her own simple, self-sacrificing life.

These three sayings of hers show the quality of her mind:

"Let us always meet each other with a smile, for a smile is the beginning of love."

"Sharing is the most important thing in the world."

"I am just a little pencil in God's hand."

THE FRIENDSHIP BOOK

OUR neighbour, Fred, was working in his garden when I passed the other day. As I greeted him, he straightened up and said, as he mopped his brow, "Eh, Francis, for this job you need a cast-iron back with a hinge in it!"

Nicely put! But then, Rudyard Kipling reminded us that ". . . gardens are not made by saying, 'Oh, how wonderful!' And sitting in the shade."

Kipling was talking, of course, not only about our ordinary gardens, but about life itself. Cast-iron backs, effort, patience are all part of the price we pay for any worthwhile achievement.

FOR where two or three are gathered together in my name, there am I in the midst of them.

Matthew 18, 20

LAURA RICHARDS is probably best known for her children's story, "The House with the Golden Windows", but she also wrote some delightful verses.

One that comes back to me over the years is about a small girl who sniffed a rose and exclaimed:

"Oh, what a pity,
I've only one nose!"

Haven't you felt like that sometimes? There is so much goodness and gladness and beauty in the world, so much to delight our senses that we feel we can scarcely take it all in.

If we *do* feel like that, then we are among the world's truly happy people.

SEPTEMBER

TUESDAY—SEPTEMBER 1.

"I HEAR your minister is leaving," said a lady to her friend when they happened to meet as they walked home from their respective churches.

"Yes," was the reply, "and we have just been given a letter asking for donations so that we can give him a little momentum."

Not quite what she meant—I hope!

WEDNESDAY—SEPTEMBER 2.

P. J. BARSBY, of Attenborough, Nottingham, sent me this charming poem which he titles "The Bride":

Modestly veiled, and gowned in lace,
An ethereal beauty of form and face,
A vision of loveliness and grace,
She stands beside her groom.

And never did a lovelier bride
Stand by a handsome bridegroom's side;
He looks at her with love and pride
This special afternoon.

What thoughts are in that pretty head
As now the marriage vows are said?
She's looking radiant, though it's said
She cried in her own room.

But as they come back up the aisle
Gone are the fears she had awhile;
There's on her face a loving smile
Shared with her handsome groom.

AUTUMN SWAN

THE FRIENDSHIP BOOK

JOHN HILLABY is a great walker as his books "Journey Through Britain" and "Journey Through Europe" show. Many are the adventures he has had, walking sometimes as much as 40 miles a day. He obviously revels in the unexpected.

Yet, in another of his books, "Journey Through Love", he makes this admission: "When I come to think of days spent in high passes of the Alps, I know that at heart, a portion of my consciousness was constantly pre-occupied with bearings and path-finding and flickers of doubt about what lay beyond the next crest. Sustained peace, as I understand it, comes from knowing exactly where I am, and for this there is much to be said for knowing a few walks extremely well."

Wise words indeed, from an adventurous spirit; and it applies to more than walking. Of course there is a place in life for adventure, for trying new things, but real peace of heart comes from the familiar things — familiar places, old friends, often-listened-to music, well-thumbed books. As the song puts it, "These are a few of my favourite things".

AS we grow older, and the years pass, suddenly we realise that the time remaining to us must be getting short. An elderly reader in Tylers Green, High Wycombe, sent me the following imaginary newspaper advertisement:

"Lost — two golden hours, each set with 60 diamond minutes. No reward is offered as they are lost for ever."

Don't lose any diamond minutes today. They are too precious.

K

THE FRIENDSHIP BOOK

FRED Dibnah is a steeplejack with a passion for steam rollers! He is a "character" in his own right, and a combination of all these things has made him into a television personality, too.

I was amused by his comment as he drove his ponderous machine at five m.p.h. along a country lane. "I find these fields and trees a bit boring. After all, one elm tree is much like another elm tree, one ash like another. Mill chimneys are not like that. Every one is different!"

How true it is that "beauty is in the eye of the beholder".

We may not understand the likes and dislikes of others, but let us be grateful for those things which bring *us* delight, and make the most of them today.

MY son, if thou come to serve the Lord, prepare thy soul for temptation.   Ecclesiasticus 2, 1

I READ somewhere of a tribe whose method of carrying small loads was to tie one to each end of a pole and then carry it across their shoulders so that the burdens balanced each other. If there was only one package, they would tie a heavy stone to the other end of the pole.

Perhaps it seems silly to carry twice as much as you need, but it really is easier that way, rather than trying to carry one burden by itself.

The lesson of this parable isn't difficult to see — carrying someone else's burden really does lighten our own.

THE FRIENDSHIP BOOK

TUESDAY—SEPTEMBER 8.

A FRIEND of ours who retired to the country takes great delight in collecting quaint and amusing turns of speech used by farmers and other country folk. One that particularly amused me was that used by an old man who was taking his dog for a walk and stopped to talk to a friend. His dog sat gazing up at them, and his master commented, "Just hark at he, looking at we wid his nose!"

WEDNESDAY—SEPTEMBER 9.

NOT long ago, the Lady of the House and I visited Malham Cove in Yorkshire and saw there on the rock, the black marks left by Tom the chimney sweep from "The Water Babies" as he slid down into the water. Of course, they aren't really soot-marks, but lichen. However, this is supposed to be part of the inspiration of Charles Kingsley's famous story. That, together with "Hereward The Wake", "The Heroes" and "Westward Ho!" must bring back many childhood memories to older readers.

Kingsley was indeed a famous and accomplished author, but there is another side of his life not often noted. For over 30 years, he served the little country church of Eversley on the borders of Hampshire and Berkshire, first as curate then as rector. His preaching filled a church which had been nearly empty when he went there. He visited every home in the parish. He formed a library, a maternity society, a loan fund, a coal club and many other societies.

When he died, there was a move to have him buried in Westminster Abbey, but his widow resisted this, knowing his wish to lie in the churchyard of the village where he had lived and worked for so long. A great author — and a very humble man!

THE FRIENDSHIP BOOK

THURSDAY—SEPTEMBER 10.

I HEARD an amusing story about a rather strict factory owner who put a notice on the wall saying, "Whenever I enter the workshop I want to see every man cheerfully performing his task. I am providing a suggestion box and invite all of you to put in ideas as to how this can be brought about."

A week later, when he opened the box, he found a slip of paper on which was written, "Take the rubber soles off your shoes!"

FRIDAY—SEPTEMBER 11.

"THERE aren't any real characters nowadays," commented an old friend recently. "Everybody seems to think alike — have the herd instinct."

As I left him I wondered if there is any truth in his remarks. Perhaps we do tend to be influenced too much by mass judgements, mass reaction, mass opinions. Perhaps it is not as easy as it used to be to defend our individuality, to be ourselves. It takes courage. It also takes a certain amount of self-knowledge and that includes acknowledging our weaknesses as well as our strength.

We tend to let harsh criticism of someone go by without defending that person who is not present to defend himself. Too often we say, "I don't want to get involved."

Do we have the courage to widen the scope of our lives? It can be done, even if we are not in the best of health or elderly.

Watching a little of the Olympic Games for the Handicapped on TV, I marvelled at the courage and tenacity shown by these young people. They were determined to overcome any handicap. They displayed character in its best sense.

THE FRIENDSHIP BOOK

MY thanks to Carol Wills for these delightful lines:

> My ears are filled with music
>   Of the song-birds overhead.
> I smell the field flowers weaving
>   Their sweet scents around my head.
> I feel a warmth embrace me
>   From the kiss of a sunbeam,
> And taste the sparkling freshness
>   Of the ice-cold mountain stream.
> My eyes are filled with wonder
>   When Nature's work I see,
> And I revel in the glory
>   That all her gifts are free.

JESUS said unto him, if thou wilt be perfect, go and sell that thou hast, and give to the poor, and thou shalt have treasure in heaven: and come and follow me.   Matthew 19, 21

THE famous artist, the late L.S. Lowry, painted many scenes of the industrial towns of North England with what used to be called their "dark satanic mills".

But have you ever noticed that the predominant colour in his paintings is not, as you might have expected, black, but *white?* There are white backgrounds, whitish-coloured sky, white roads and pavements.

It is as though Lowry found a brightness where others saw only soot and gloom.

THE FRIENDSHIP BOOK

JOSEPH COOPER, the musician, became well-known to millions through his television programme "Face The Music". In his autobiography he tells how, as a schoolboy in Bristol, he went to hear the pianist Rachmaninoff play at a concert in the Colton Hall. He writes, "I couldn't believe that Rachmaninoff was actually playing on an ordinary piano, the sound was so superb."

He was sitting on the platform behind the performer so, at the end of the concert, with schoolboy curiosity, he touched a few notes on the piano before being moved off by an irate official.

"But," says Cooper, "I found it was just a beautiful Steinway concert grand, nothing different about it — it was the magic that Rachmaninoff himself was putting into it."

I wonder how often it occurs to us that, ordinary though we may be, *we* can put magic into the things we do. Our personality, our enthusiasm, our love are all part of this mysterious quality which can transform something quite ordinary into a thing of real beauty.

"LOOK at that!" our old friend Mary almost snorted, as she took a bottle of sauce from her shopping basket and pointed at the label which said the contents were enriched by "a secret blend of herbs".

"When I have a good recipe," she said, "I don't keep it secret. I share it with as many people as I can."

Well, I suppose trade secrets are one thing and Mary's recipes quite another. But if there is something we have enjoyed — whether a recipe, a good book or an amusing story, we can get and give a lot of pleasure by sharing it with others.

CONCENTRATION

THE FRIENDSHIP BOOK

WE sometimes use or hear the words, "I worried myself sick", and indeed doctors and psychologists assure us that worry *can* affect our physical well-being.

A friend of ours, who always manages to keep cheerful in circumstances which would have depressed most people, once said to me, "Well, you see, Francis, I don't believe in worrying myself sick; I believe in hoping myself healthy!"

A quaint way of putting it, perhaps, but hopefulness certainly works for him, and it can for us, too.

THE 17th century religious writer Jeremy Taylor wrote: "Enjoy the blessings of this day if God sends them—for this day only is ours; we are dead to yesterday and we are not born to tomorrow."

The Indian poet Kabidasa who lived in the third century wrote:

> *Look to this day for it is life,*
> *The very life of life;*
> *In its brief course lie all*
> *The verities and realities of your existence.*

William Wordsworth knew this and in his "Guide to the Lakes" he wrote, "It has been said that in human life there are moments worth ages. In a more subdued tone of sympathy may we affirm, that in the climate of England there are, for the lover of nature, days which are worth whole months, I might say, even years."

From personal experience we all know the rich satisfaction that comes from a day well spent, either in work or leisure. Let us be grateful for every single minute of this wonderful day.

THE FRIENDSHIP BOOK

AMONG her treasures the Lady of the House numbers, of all things, a tiny foil mince-pie dish. A strange "treasure", you may think. But some years ago, in hospital, she was delighted when a neighbour's child brought the little pie she had baked herself as a "get-well" gift. The dish is of no value, of course, but the memories it arouses make it a particularly special possession.

It is rather like the jug which thousands of visitors to Bedford Museum must have seen — the jug (a very ordinary one) in which John Bunyan's wife used to carry soup for her husband when he was in prison. I called it "ordinary", but indeed it isn't!

HONOUR all men. Love the brotherhood. Fear God. Honour the king.   1 Peter 2, 17

A MOTHER and her ten-year-old son were standing in front of Tintoretto's famous painting of the Nativity.

Little Peter remarked: "Mummy, I can never understand all that business about the manger. After all, Jesus was God's Son, wasn't he, and surely God could have done better than to have had his son born in a dirty old stable?"

"Well," replied his mother, "you must remember that his parents were a long way from home, and the whole town was packed out with other travellers, and they were very poor."

"They can't have been so very poor," Peter interrupted, "to get themselves painted by someone like Tintoretto!"

THE FRIENDSHIP BOOK

WHEN I was a small boy, one of the great events in the life of the church I attended was the annual Missionary Weekend when, among the various activities and exhibitions, was a visit by a missionary from abroad.

On one occasion, the missionary was from China. "I wonder if you boys ever fight?" he asked, and then said, "let me tell you about a Chinese fight." He explained that a friend had been showing him various habits and customs and had taken him to see a "Chinese fight".

Two men were jabbering away to each other, obviously very angry. This went on for some time and the crowd which had gathered to watch was getting very excited. But nothing else happened—nothing that looked like a *fight*.

The explanation was this: the two men had had a quarrel and were arguing the matter out, saying all sorts of insulting things about each other. Inevitably, sooner or later one of them would lose his temper completely and strike a blow at the other man.

The man who struck the first blow would be said to have lost the fight!

THE well-known author and physician, Paul Tournier, says in "A Doctor's Casebook" that patients sometimes thank him for what they call his patience in listening to everything they tell him, but then he goes on to admit, "It is not patience at all; it is interest."

Of course, Paul Tournier has considerable medical skill, too, but who can doubt that it is this interest in people which made him a great doctor?

THE FRIENDSHIP BOOK

A N elderly Quaker woman with a beautiful complexion was asked what kind of cosmetic she used. Smilingly, she offered this prescription: " I use truth for my lips; for my voice, prayer; for my eyes, pity; for my hands, charity; for my figure, uprightness; for my heart, love. This prescription incurs no expense, and the supply will be increased with continued use."

W ILLIAM SHAKESPEARE said that we could find, "tongues in trees, books in the running brooks, sermons in stones", but I confess I never thought of finding a sermon in a bottle of Coca-Cola, yet that is just what a visiting preacher to our church did recently!

He explained that in certain parts of West Africa, it is still the custom to offer a visitor a bowl containing cola nuts which are about the size of a chestnut and break into segments just like an orange does. Visitors then place the pieces in their right hand and offer them round the room to everyone present, and then when the pieces have been handed out, they are eaten by everyone together as a sign of friendship.

The preacher told us, too, that near Lagos, there is a boys' boarding school with the name *Igbobi* which translated means The Place of the Cola Nuts — the Place of Friendship.

I don't think I shall ever see a bottle of Coke again without remembering that sermon — which no doubt is what the preacher intended. However, it will do more than remind me of the sermon, it will remind me that true friendship and fellowship are the important things in life.

THE FRIENDSHIP BOOK

OUR friend, Millicent Brown, works in a local library and often makes us smile with the remarks of borrowers — such as the lady who was looking for what she called a "non-friction book". Recently, another lady had filled in the necessary card so that the library could retain a book which was out on loan. "Will you preserve this book, for me, please?" she asked.

Not quite what she meant! Yet in a sense, she had a point. I am sure we all have books we want preserved — we would be sad if, for example, we lent, and then lost track of them. We have all read books whose contents lie stored in our minds. Long may they be preserved!

FOR thine incorruptible Spirit is in all things.

Wisdom 12, 1

DR DONALD SOPER, the Methodist minister and Life Peer, often paid tribute to the firm but kindly religious upbringing which clearly had so great an influence on his life.

He used to tell how, when the family went on their annual seaside holiday, the first thing they did after arrival at their holiday resort on Saturday was to hunt out the local Wesleyan church where they would worship as a family the following day. Only after that were the children allowed to dash off to the beach to play.

In this gentle way the young Sopers were not allowed to forget that holidays were originally holy days.

PRETTY PUSS

Why are you staring, pussy?
  What is the thing you see?
It isn't a mouse or a squirrel
  Or a little bird in a tree.

What are you seeing, pussy?
  Something tasty for tea?
Whatever it is you think is there,
  I wish you would look at ME!

THE FRIENDSHIP BOOK

YOUNG Billy tried out his latest riddle on me the other day.

"Why is a rock braver than a mountain, Mr Gay?" I shook my head. "Because it's a little boulder!"

"LATE Autumn" is the title of this charming poem by Violet Hall:

> The straw has been baled
>   And all carted away,
> The apples are rosy,
>   The hedgerow is gay
> With amethyst berries
>   That purple the lips,
> And sour matt-bloomed sloes
>   And glossy red hips.
>
> Bright is the Autumn
>   When spiked conkers fall,
> To be captured by schoolboys
>   In no time at all;
> When trees are aflame
>   With amber and gold,
> And squirrels are scrabbling
>   For nuts in the mould.
>
> The beechmast lies thick
>   O'er the moist woodland bed,
> As hedgehog goes hunting
>   A rest for his head;
> To curl up for winter
>   Before it's too late —
> Ere ice seals the duck-pond,
>   And frost gems the gate.

OCTOBER

THURSDAY—OCTOBER 1.

THE Lady of the House had said she was going to have a "quiet day", so I was surprised when I returned home and found her busily cleaning the insides of all the windows.

"I thought you were going to have a break," I said.

"I know, Francis," she replied, "but the window-cleaner came this morning and when he had left the outsides so bright and sparkling, I felt I just had to make the insides match."

Isn't that a clear demonstration of the power of example!

FRIDAY—OCTOBER 2.

WILLIAM HENRY HUDSON, the writer and naturalist, was born in South America, but is best remembered for his love of the English countryside. To him, the surroundings of country churches were places of refreshment for tired limbs, and inspired much of his writing. He always regarded a country churchyard as "a shaded fountain in a desert", giving a sense of enduring peace.

He used to spend every winter in Cornwall, and whilst preparing his book, he stayed in the village of Zennor. There he so impressed the local folk that after his death they erected a stone with the simple inscription, "W.H. Hudson often came here".

His grave on the Sussex Downs bears this lovely epitaph which epitomises his feeling for the countryside to which he had come as a stranger: "He loved birds and green places and the wind on the heath, and saw the brightness of the skirts of God".

THE FRIENDSHIP BOOK

PERHAPS you remember the song that went "I'm busy doing nothing, nothing the whole day through . . ."

It makes it sound so easy. Yet really, if you've ever tried, you'll know just how difficult it is to be idle!

The writer J. B. Priestley summed up his thoughts on the matter in a little piece entitled "Can you idle?" He wrote:

"Any man can be fussy and rid himself of energy all over the place, but a man has to have something in him before he can settle down to do nothing. He must have reserves to draw upon, must be able to plunge into strange slow rivers of dream and reverie, must be at heart a poet".

I think I'd rather keep busy!

TO every thing there is a season, and a time to every purpose under the heaven.   Ecclesiastes 3, 1

HERE is a very unusual poem sent to me by Mrs Eleanor K. Pratt of Leyburn, North Yorkshire. It's called "A Swarm of B's":

> B hopeful, B happy, B cheerful, B kind,
> B Busy of Body, B modest of mind,
> B earnest, B truthful, B firm and B good,
> B sure your B haviour B all that it should.
>
> B sharp in the morning, and never B flat,
> B ware most of all that you never B that,
> B all of these things and whatever B fall,
> B sure you'll B happy and B loved By us all!

THE FRIENDSHIP BOOK

ONE day, Ted Yorke, a Londoner, had to visit the out patients' department of a hospital. While he sat rather gloomily waiting his turn, his attention was caught by a notice on one of the doors.

It read: "Smile, please. We, too, have problems."

He couldn't help it. He started smiling!

Sometimes it's too easy to think that we have all the worries and others have none. Ted tells me he'll try not to think that way again. Will you?

THE parishioners of Morwenstow, in Cornwall, in the middle of last century, must often have shaken their heads in wonderment at the eccentric behaviour of their vicar, the Rev. Stephen Hawker, who walked about the parish in the strangest attire, held services to which cats and dogs were specially invited to bring their owners, and built chimneys on his vicarage in the shape of church towers!

Yet all this, and perhaps Stephen Hawker himself, might have been forgotten but for his one great inspiration — the Harvest Festival.

On the first Sunday in October, 1843, he invited his parishioners to a special service "to give thanks to God for the fruits of harvest."

No doubt many of his critics dismissed this as just another of Parson Hawker's idiosyncrasies — but not so. Not only was his service an outstanding success, but the idea caught on, and by 1862, when the Convocation of Canterbury issued a special Order of Service for such occasions, the practice was widespread throughout England.

We might give Parson Hawker a thought when we sing our harvest hymns.

L

THE FRIENDSHIP BOOK

I LIKE the story of the country vicar who was so anxious to please the visiting Duke of Wellington, that he asked the victor of Waterloo if there was anything particular he wished the Sunday sermon to be about. "Yes, about ten minutes," replied the Duke.

FOR most of us, I suppose, it is meals that divide up the day. For the monks of mediaeval times, it was the eight services, three before daybreak — Matins, Lauds and Prime, with others — Tierce, Sext, None — at three-hourly intervals, Vespers at sunset, and Compline just before going to bed.

It is a pattern few would have the stamina or the desire to follow, but in her familiar hymn, "Lord of all hopefulness, Lord of all joy", Jan Struther has captured a similar idea which I think can be meaningful in this modern world. Do you remember the closing lines of each verse?

"Your bliss in our hearts, Lord, at the break of the day."

"Your strength in our hearts, Lord, at the noon of the day."

"Your love in our hearts, Lord, at the eve of the day."

"Your peace in our hearts, Lord, at the close of the day."

Whether we pray or not, these are good thoughts to have at each period of the day. We talk of living a day at a time. There's something to be said, too, I think, for dividing the day in this sort of way and living it a bit at a time!

THE FRIENDSHIP BOOK

I KNEW a hearing-aid specialist who, because he is severely deaf himself, understands the problems faced by his patients.

"Look at these," he said one day. "Like little ears, aren't they? They are moulds taken from the ear to provide an exact impression. Now I'm going to send them away so that hearing-aids can be made with them. Oh, I know what you are thinking. It's sad that people need them. Sad but wonderful!

"When the moulds come back they will be attached to battery-operated appliances," he explained. "Then children will hear the birds singing and all the other wonderful sounds that normal people take for granted.

"What's more," he added, "100 years ago, or less, such children would never have had a proper chance in life simply because they could not hear properly. Now scientific miracles enable them to live full and happy lives."

I left him, paying new attention to the sounds all around me.

A WISE son heareth his father's instruction: but a scorner heareth not rebuke.   Proverbs 13,1

WE sometimes say, "Love is blind", but I think the American poet, Phoebe Cary, was much nearer to the truth when she wrote,

> I think true love is never blind,
>   But rather brings an added light,
> An inner vision quick to find
>   The beauties hid from common sight.

ANCIENT ROAD

Straight as a column of soldiers,
Emperor Hadrian built his wall.
A barrier once — now peace prevails;
Only the wind blows echoes of Gaul.

THE FRIENDSHIP BOOK

WE all admire the skill of the sheepdogs as displayed on the TV programme "One Man and His Dog". I suppose, though, few of us stop to give a word of praise to the sheep.

One person who does is Viv Billingham. Viv and her husband are shepherds in the Cheviot Hills and you may have seen Viv taking part in competitions and holding her own with the men.

Sheep are thought of as foolish creatures, but that is very far from the truth, she tells us in her book "One Woman and Her Dog". Given time to gather their thoughts they are capable of great wisdom and quick action.

She has seen a mother charging with head down like a bull when her lamb's safety was threatened. Another attacked and killed a snake in defence of her offspring.

Viv is no sentimentalist, but her hours in the company of animals of every sort have taught her how slender is the line that divides them from us.

She loves her clever dogs, but she loves, too, her humble, patient sheep.

IN his book, "The Magic of Thinking Big", Dr David Schwartz tells of a friend of his who, though having only one arm, was an excellent golfer. Schwartz once said to him, "You know there are plenty of golfers with two arms who can't play nearly as well as you. How have you managed to develop your skill in spite of your handicap?"

His friend replied, "It's my experience that the right attitude and one arm will beat the wrong attitude and two arms every time!"

THE FRIENDSHIP BOOK

I LIKE this poem sent to me by Jean Forrest of Cleveland:

> I heard a robin sing today,
>   His note was sweet and clear,
> He stood upon my windowsill
>   And filled my heart with cheer.
>
> Today was dark and dreary,
>   And it seemed as if he knew
> That I was sitting all alone
>   And feeling rather blue.
>
> His eyes were black and shining,
>   And scarlet was his coat,
> As, heedless of the icy wind,
>   His song poured from his throat.
>
> My ears were filled with silver sounds,
>   My head was light and gay,
> But when I tried to talk to him
>   He quickly flew away.

WHEN Florence Nightingale was sailing to the Crimea with her first batch of volunteer nurses, the girls were talking excitedly about the adventure on which they were embarking. But Florence Nightingale had another angle to put to them, "Young women," she said, "The strongest will be wanted at the washtub!"

Not much adventure about that! But do *we* forget sometimes the important part we have to play as we undertake what the poet George Herbert called, "the daily round, the trivial task"?

THE FRIENDSHIP BOOK

THE evangelist Billy Graham was talking to an eager student at a theological college. The young man, tired of lectures, was impatient to get on with the pursuit of his career. "The world's in a bad shape," he argued. "Why should I waste more time just training?"

Graham replied quietly, "If you were told to cut down trees in a wood, but the axe given you was blunt — though made of good steel — would you not spend some valuable time sharpening it?"

THE Lord is gracious, and merciful: long-suffering, and of great goodness.   Psalm 145, 8

I READ somewhere that Charles Blondin, the famous French "King of the Tightrope", was frightened of falling only a few times in his career.

His worst experience was when he walked a tightrope suspended between the masts of a ship on a voyage to India. Then he was almost petrified. For one thing, he was feeling very sea-sick, and for another, a heavy swell had started. However, the rope was fixed, and the event was for charity, so Blondin started his walk with the surging sea below. He got across safely, though it took him longer to complete than he had planned. But what an effort it had been to overcome his fear!

Few of us are called upon to display such physical courage as this famous tightrope-walker, or even the kind regularly practised by circus performers, yet every day amidst disasters and fires there are reports of gallant rescues and the bravery of ordinary folk. We can all be heroes in many quiet ways.

THE FRIENDSHIP BOOK

WHAT a store of wise and witty sayings Mark Twain left us. After many years' acquaintance with his writings I still come across ones new to me. For example, "A millionaire's money is twice tainted — 'Taint mine and 'Taint yours!"

How right Mark Twain was! There is nothing that so taints our outlook on life or on other people, as envy and jealousy. Gratitude and contentment are the surest ways to lasting happiness.

SOMETIMES when we visit our old friend Mary she quickly puts her hymn-book down and says half-apologetically, "I was just singing to myself."

Well, Mary has no need to apologise. Probably many of us do the same, finding much help in our heritage of hymns. Dr John Mason Neale to whom we owe the English translation of such well-known hymns as "All glory, laud and honour", "O come, O come Emmanuel", "Jerusalem the golden", "O happy band of pilgrims" and many others, once said that he did not believe in the copyrighting of hymns. "A hymn," he said, "the moment it is published, ought to become the common property of Christendom, the author retaining no private right in it whatever."

Perhaps not everyone will agree with that, yet in a real sense don't we feel that the great hymns of the Church *do* belong to us? Hymn-singing sessions on radio and television are still among the most popular of programmes. We have indeed a great heritage through hymn-writers of all sections of the Church — Anglican, Roman Catholic, Presbyterian, Methodist, Baptist to mention but a few. Let's go on singing them, not only in public, but to ourselves, as Mary does.

THE FRIENDSHIP BOOK

DR SAMUEL JOHNSON, the 18th century writer, is perhaps best-known for the famous dictionary he compiled. Among his contemporaries, he often appeared an awe-inspiring figure, devastating in his wit, criticism and intellectual power.

When he died, another side of his character was discovered, for in his private diary were found many prayers and meditations written for his own use and showing him to be a man of great humility.

One of his prayers goes, "Make me to remember, O God, that every day is Thy gift, and ought to be used according to Thy command. Grant me, therefore, so to repent of my negligence that I may obtain mercy from Thee, and pass the time which Thou shalt yet allow me in diligent performance of Thy commands."

Again, he prays, "enlighten my understanding with knowledge of right . . . that I may always endeavour to do good and hinder evil."

We ought not to be surprised at this aspect of Samuel Johnson's life. True greatness and true humility invariably go together.

ALMOST every day in life I see Donald Wilson swing down the road, giving a cheerful "Good Morning" to everybody he meets, even complete strangers.

We have a new neighbour, and the other day she said to Donald's wife, "Please tell your husband that the cheerful way he says 'Good morning' makes me feel better all day."

A cheerful word is never wasted. It often travels farther than we think.

THE FRIENDSHIP BOOK

THE celebrated violinist Niccolo Paganini was born on this day in 1782.

The first time that he appeared in Paris, many of France's noble citizens and gentry gathered to hear him play. He began to tune his instrument — and one of the strings broke. Moments later a second string broke, then a third.

Paginini paused, took a deep breath, then raised the violin again. And from the sole remaining string, the G string, he drew forth what was to become one of his most popular works, the *Sonata Napoleone.*

The concert, which started in disaster, ended in triumph, thanks to the young Paginini's courage and resourcefulness.

FOR with thee is the well of life: and in thy light shall we see light.   Psalm 36, 9

WE know that we have five senses — sight, hearing, touch, taste and smell — but we don't always make full use of them. In his book, "The Inner Sentinel", Dr L. P. Jacks says that most of us are dominated largely by sight.

He tells of an experiment in which students were put in a room for two minutes, then asked to report on everything they had observed.

In almost every case, it was only things they had *seen* which they recorded — not the smell of cooking from an adjacent room, for example, or even the sound of a band in the street below!

It's a reminder to us of how much there is to enjoy if we let *all* our senses have a chance.

THE FRIENDSHIP BOOK

I LIKE this little anonymous verse I came across recently:

> *Kind hearts are the garden,*
> *Kind thoughts are the roots;*
> *Kind words are the blossoms,*
> *Kind deeds are the fruits.*

THE Chinese have a legend about a boy who had played chess from a very early age and become so proficient, that by the time he was 12 he was counted good enough to play against the chess champion of the whole of China.

It was a great day for him, and greater still when, after only two hours, he defeated the champion. Then, according to the legend, a genie appeared and said to the boy, Wan Sung, "It is very clever of you to have beaten the champion, and I am going to give you one wish as a reward. Whatever you wish, I will grant you."

Wan Sung thought for a moment and then said, "I would like to have these two hours all over again." So it happened, and at the end of the game, the genie appeared again, because, after all, he had been part of what happened in the first two hours. Once more, he gave Wan Sung a wish, and *again* he wished to have the last two hours over again. It happened — again, and again! Presumably he is still playing that game, and is no doubt sick to death of it by now!

It's only a story of course, but isn't it also a lesson about the folly of wanting to bring back the past? It's now, today, that counts.

As the Sanskrit poet wrote, "Look well, therefore, to this day."

THE FRIENDSHIP BOOK

A few weeks ago, the Lady of the House took two little girls to the station to meet a friend who was coming home from holiday.

Whilst waiting for the train, the five-year-old carefully examined all the surroundings, and spent a long time gazing at the roof.

At last she came back to my friend and asked, "What's wrong with the station?"

"What do you mean?" asked my friend.

"Well," said the little girl, "at Sunday School we always pray, 'Lead us not into the station' . . !"

THERE is a story of an old German schoolmaster who, when he entered his class in the morning, used to take off his cap and bow to the boys. When he was asked why he did this he replied, "You never know what one of those boys may one day become."

How right he was! One of them was called Martin Luther.

Having read that, let us look today with new eyes at the children we meet in our homes, or in the street . . . seeing them as Wordsworth did, "trailing clouds of glory . . ."!

RECENTLY, I came on two sayings which remind me that there must be real compassion and love behind everything we do.

The novelist, George Eliot, wrote, "If you feel no love, sit still." And Rabindranath Tagore, the Indian poet and philosopher, said, "He who tries to do good stands knocking at the door, but he who loves, finds the door open."

NOVEMBER

SUNDAY—NOVEMBER 1.

ESCHEW evil, do good, seek peace, and ensue it.
Psalm 34, 14

MONDAY—NOVEMBER 2.

ONE of the loveliest hymns which has reached us from Asia, begins:

> One who is all unfit to count
> As scholar in Thy school . . .

Its writer was an Indian poet who one day had been travelling in a train with an Englishman. They chatted in a very friendly way, without the Englishman showing any of the signs of superiority which many Europeans were accustomed to do then.

When they reached their destination, the Englishman gave his friend a copy of The New Testament and urged him to study it.

The Indian had been so impressed by his companion's courtesy and friendliness that he began to read the book. It gripped him, with its words of love, tenderness and truth, and not long afterwards, he was baptised as a Christian.

Narayan Vaman Tilak later wrote his beautiful hymn, one that would never have been and whose writer would never have become a Christian, had it not been for the simple courtesy of a man whose name we do not kow.

Not every thoughtful action will have this kind of result, but it's always true that goodness grows from goodness.

THE FRIENDSHIP BOOK

OUR friend Mary makes her own Christmas puddings, and several for her friends, too. The other day when the Lady of the House and I called, she was busily weighing out the ingredients on the old scales which, she proudly tells us, her mother used when she was making *her* Christmas puddings—the sort with weights on one side and a pan for ingredients on the other.

"You know, Francis," she said, "I always preach a little sermon to myself when I am using these scales." She placed some weights on. "That's my arthritis, my deafness and aches and pains." She poured flour into the scale pan. "That's some of the blessings I have—friends, books, a comfortable house. See how the scale goes down with a bang!"

A new way, indeed, of counting our blessings!

ISOBEL W. HUTCHINSON, who lived in West Lothian, Scotland, wrote many lovely poems, of which this is one:

> I don't know where I go in sleep,
> But I go far away
> From little troubled noisy things,
> Loudnesses of the day,
> And like a bird that seeks her nest
> My soul spreads wing and finds her rest.
>
> I don't know what I hear in sleep,
> But afterwards it sings,
> And sometimes in the day I meet
> Strange half-remembered things
> That stretch a faint elusive hand
> Of greeting from some Fatherland.

THE FRIENDSHIP BOOK

THURSDAY—NOVEMBER 5.

A LL over our land tonight, the sky will be lit with the glow of thousands of bonfires.

I have never seen our neighbour, Lucy Holmes, at our local bonfire, so I was rather surprised to hear her say the other day, "I love Bonfire Night!"

"You do?" I queried.

"Yes," she replied. "It gives me a chance to clear out so much old rubbish for the youngsters to burn!"

Well, that's another value of the bonfire, I suppose.

While we are at it, we might well have a little "mental bonfire" of our own, clearing out some of the "rubbish" — the grumbles, grudges, needless worries, bitter memories and so much else that clutters up our minds. Have a bonfire!

FRIDAY—NOVEMBER 6.

I WONDER if, like me, when you find yourself lost in an unfamiliar place and enquire the way, you often get the answer, "I'm sorry, I'm a stranger here myself." There must be an awful lot of strangers about!

A friend of ours who went recently to live in a distant town, very quickly settled in to a church there. He was attracted to it, he told me, because on the board outside it said, "THERE ARE NO STRANGERS HERE". He found it was true; everybody made him welcome and he felt at home straight away.

We may not always be able to tell people the way when they ask us, but what a great contribution we could all make to other people's happiness if we did our bit to ensure that in our various groups and activities "there are no strangers here".

DAY'S END

THE FRIENDSHIP BOOK

THERE was once an extra smile for those who read a Wayside Pulpit notice outside a chapel in the Rhondda Valley. "Love thy neighbour", said the printed message, but underneath, someone had written: "I can't — I know him!"

FOR many are called, but few are chosen.

Matthew 22, 14

I LIKE to visit the office of my friend, Alistair Cowan, not only because he always has such a cheerful welcome however busy he may be, but also because of what he calls his "Thought for the Week".

This is a card which he pins over his desk on which he writes some inspiring thought which has helped him and which he hopes may help others. They have certainly often helped me.

Recently, it was a verse from one of Dr. Norman Vincent Peale's books:

If you think you are beaten, you are;
If you think you dare not, you don't,
If you want to win, but think you can't
It's almost sure you won't.
If you think you'll lose, you're lost;
For out in the world we find
Success begins with a person's will;
It's all in the state of mind.
Life's battles don't always go
To the stronger and faster man,
But sooner or later the man who wins
Is the man who thinks he can.

M

THE FRIENDSHIP BOOK

TUESDAY—NOVEMBER 10.

IT was a lovely wedding. The sun was shining, the bride was radiant and everything was going without a hitch until the vicar announced Hymn 540. There was dead silence. The organist was seen to shake his head. What was wrong?

The vicar checked his sheet again. "Oh, I'm sorry," he said. "Hymn 520, 'Love Divine, all loves excelling.' Hymn 540 is, 'Fight the good fight'!"

WEDNESDAY—NOVEMBER 11.

ONE day during the last century, a small lady was walking in a Yorkshire village when she met a shy little boy and greeted him kindly. The boy never forgot that encounter, for the lady was the writer, Charlotte Brontë from Haworth Parsonage.

James Roberts was the boy, and he belonged to a poor family, but like so many Victorians he studied and worked hard until he became a wealthy textile manufacturer. He maintained a lifelong interest in the Brontë family and The Brontë Society.

At first the Society's possessions were housed above a bank, but in the late 1920's, the Old Parsonage — the former home of the famous family — came up for sale. Sir James Roberts (as he then was) bought it, and in 1929 it was officially opened by his wife.

Of course, since those days, Haworth Parsonage has been wonderfully improved and has a fine extension, but the original part carefully resembles its appearance when the Brontës used the rooms. Over 200,000 people now visit the building each year.

The fame of the Parsonage Museum is worldwide, but how many tourists, I wonder, know that it owes its existence to the smile Charlotte gave to a little boy in the street.

THE FRIENDSHIP BOOK

THIS fine and comforting poem requires no explanation from me:

One who is there to intercede,
One who helps you in your need;
One who has a soothing power,
Calming you in darkest hour.
One who shares your grief and pain,
And when rebuffed, comes back again;
One who knows your every mood,
Does not condemn, does not intrude.
One who shares your happiness
As well as sorrow and distress.
One who's with you to the end.
Won't you let Him be your friend?

LEONARD PENDLEBURY, a retired Merchant Navy officer, went to live in his native West Country, where he used to give occasional broadcasts.

In one of these he told of a junior officer who had spent the entire day working hard, loading cargo on a ship berthed in Sydney Harbour. As the sun went down, the temperature dropped sharply, and by the time he stopped, he felt tired, cold and more than a bit fed-up with himself, the ship and the world at large.

As he passed the Chief Officer, the senior man smiled and said, "You have certainly done a good day's work!"

Over 50 years later, Leonard Pendlebury still remembered those few words which not only lifted his spirits that evening, but helped him decide to stay on in the Merchant Navy and make it his career.

A word of appreciation can go a long, long way.

THE FRIENDSHIP BOOK

SATURDAY—NOVEMBER 14.

CHARLES DARWIN sat at the desk in his study, hard at work. It was a rule of the house that the great man must not be disturbed while he was writing, but suddenly the door opened and a chubby four-year-old peeped in, and said solemnly, "Daddy, if you'll come out and play, I'll give you sixpence."

Darwin got up from his desk, took his son's hand and went out into the garden. His work could wait. He knew what was important in life — and I'm sure he didn't take that sixpence!

SUNDAY—NOVEMBER 15.

THE Lord looked down from heaven upon the children of men, to see if there were any that would understand, and seek after God.   Psalm 14, 2

MONDAY—NOVEMBER 16.

QUITE recently, I heard what seemed a very illuminating definition of goodness given by a lay preacher. She stressed that we should always be ready to put a blanket over our irritation, bad temper or impatience.

What she said started a train of thought about blankets. They are warm and cosy, but they can be used to smother a fire and they can be laid over any of the small smouldering flames of resentment that are so often sparked off in life.

A blanket of forgetfulness can be used to smother hurt feelings when we feel unappreciated or misunderstood.

Then there's the blanket of reassurance which we can wrap around the shoulders of those in doubt and children in need of comfort.

Blankets have many uses, haven't they?

THE FRIENDSHIP BOOK

THE placard in the sports shop window read: WE MAKE WEEKENDS.

Well, certainly sporting events now dominate weekends for many people. But snappy as that slogan may be, its writer is thousands of years out of date. The "weekend" was invented when, in the story of the Creation of the world, God laboured for six days and rested on the seventh. That was the very first and the very greatest weekend.

ISN'T it a lovely day?" commented a lady in the bus queue one sunny November morning.

"Oh, we'll pay for it — we're bound to have snow, sleet or fog before the week's out," came the reply from her friend.

It's a good philosophy to enjoy the present whether it brings sunshine, bird song or some stroke of luck, yet so many people seem unable to do this because they fear something will come to spoil it. I think we are all a bit like this at times.

The ancient Greek Polycrates thought along these lines. He was so scared of his happiness that he decided to give a gift to the gods, and flung a valuable ring into the sea as a sacrifice.

Not long afterwards, so the legend tells, Polycrates was given a fine, newly-caught fish. To his horror, when it was gutted, there was his ring! Polycrates decided the gods had rejected it and some terrible disaster would follow.

It's only a story, but there is a grain of truth behind it, isn't there? Why mar happiness by anticipating disaster? Or as the old saying goes: "Don't trouble trouble until trouble troubles you."

THE FRIENDSHIP BOOK

I CAME across this Chinese proverb the other day: "Let every man sweep the snow from his own doors and not busy himself with the frost on his neighbour's tiles". It's so easy to get involved in someone else's affairs, and to neglect our own, or to interfere in something which doesn't concern us at all.

It's a proverb I shall certainly be keeping in mind.

VISITORS to York Minster in the early 19th century may have paused to watch an artist busily sketching. He was John Brown, a local man, who was fascinated by the beauty of the cathedral.

To make sure his drawings were accurate, he would look up again and again towards the bosses in the centre vault of the nave, each of which carried a cameo scene from either the life of Christ or Mary.

As John drew, he never imagined how valuable his work would be. In 1840, a fire broke out in the nave and the damage included the wooden centre vault and the bosses.

During one of his visits to the Minster area after the fire, John heard an amazing thing. By some mistake or neglect, there were no designs of eight of the bosses and it was thought they could not be re-created.

Rather nervously John approached the Dean and Chapter. Might his sketches help? To his delight the drawings proved of great assistance, and because of the hobby he considered unimportant, new bosses were created with the old designs upon them.

Because John Brown had taken great care to do the job properly, the restoration was possible. There's a lesson there for all of us.

THE FRIENDSHIP BOOK

THE other Sunday our order of service had as its text for the week those familiar words of St Paul, "I have not yet reached perfection, but I press on . . ."

Strangely enough, that very same week I read an interview with the disabled violinist, Itzach Perlman, who said, "No musician ever 'peaks'. Always there is a new height of excellence to be striven after and achieved."

I pressed on a bit harder that week.

SALVATION belongeth unto the Lord: and thy blessing is upon thy people.   Psalm 3, 8

I HAVE always been fascinated by the origin of words and so was interested to learn how the expression "listless" came about.

Apparently, it is a nautical term from the days of sailing ships. When the wind fills the sails, a ship takes on a list; the only time this does not occur is when there is no wind at all and the vessel becomes "listless" — our word for dull or lifeless.

Sometimes we need a bit of wind to stir us up, as Charles Kingsley realised when he wrote his "Ode to the North-east Wind":

> *Welcome, wild North-easter!*
> *Shame it is to see*
> *Odes to every zephyr;*
> *Ne'er a verse to thee.*

At times only the "winds of adversity" can stir our listlessness. So, welcome the wind!

THE FRIENDSHIP BOOK

MANY years ago, Cecil Hunt published a collection of "Uncommon Prayers" — simple, beautiful, taken from past and present times, and from all around the world.

Among them was what he described as "A Grace told to me in Scotland many years ago." Here it is:

> *No ordinary meal — a sacrament awaits us*
> *On our tables daily spread,*
> *For men are risking lives on sea and land*
> *That we may dwell in safety and be fed.*

Saying grace is not as common a custom as it once was, but we might well take a moment to repeat these words silently in our hearts.

TODAY is the feast day of St Catherine of Alexandria, best-known perhaps through the fireworks, Catherine Wheels, which recall the fact that she is said to have been tortured on a spiked wheel.

Although there is little historical evidence about the saint, a number of interesting customs have grown up surrounding her. In some places, particularly Somerset, St Catherine's Eve and Day were celebrated as Catterntide. Because she was the patron saint of lace-makers, a table was covered with a lace cloth and on it were placed lighted candles decorated with ivy — the flames to lighten the Winter and the ivy to give promise of the Spring.

In this often dark and depressing month of November, I like to visualise that cheerful symbol of the candle and the ivy, remembering those familiar words of Shelley, "If Winter comes, can Spring be far behind?"

HAPPY LANDINGS

Remember the sledging?
The thrill of the spill,
The long trudge afterwards, back up the hill?
Wasn't it fun out there in the snow,
Smiling and laughing, our faces aglow!

THE FRIENDSHIP BOOK

WE shall have to wait a few weeks yet before our Christmas turkeys, but today in the USA is Turkey Day — officially Thanksgiving Day, recalling the feast which the first settlers celebrated when, after a disastrous Winter and anxious Spring and Summer, the harvest prospered.

It is a great festival and celebration with turkey and pumpkin pie, but the poet, Marion Douglas, reminded her fellow-Americans how to get the best out of it:

Said old gentleman Jay, "On a Thanksgiving Day,
If you want a good time, then give something away."

True of any celebration, isn't it?

THE name of the Rev. W. Colvin Williams was probably known to few people outside the small American town where he was minister. Williams was blinded by an exploding land-mine during the Last War, but he did not allow this to stop him from fulfilling his cherished ambition to train as a minister for the church he loved.

When he was ordained he said, "I feel my blindness may actually be an asset in my work. I can never judge by appearances and be prejudiced. My blindness keeps me from cutting myself off from a person because of the way he looks. I want to be the kind of person to whom anyone can come and feel secure to express himself."

I would like to have met the Rev. W. Colvin Williams.

THE FRIENDSHIP BOOK

WHAT is your favourite colour? P. J. Barsby of Attenborough, Nottingham, wrote to tell me what his is and why:

> *Blue — the colour of sunny skies*
> *And of a new-born baby's eyes;*
> *Of magic distances and space,*
> *Of placid seas and dress of lace;*
> *Of kingfisher, and blue tit, too,*
> *Who proudly flaunt their heavenly blue;*
> *Of smiling bluebells in a wood*
> *On Summer eve when life is good.*
> *No other colour is so kind*
> *As blue for bringing peace of mind.*

IN the beginning God created the heaven and the earth.   Genesis 1, 1

DURING the television broadcast of the Queen's Coronation, one of the commentators used the phrase, "the lonely dignity of majesty". And it struck many people that, in spite of the cheering crowds, there was a touching loneliness about that small, slim figure.

It reminded me, reading it again, of one of the saddest sentences I ever heard — the words of Queen Victoria after the death of her beloved Prince Albert: "There is no one to call me Victoria now."

How fortunate we are if we have someone who — in love, in friendship, in sympathy and understanding — can call us by our name.

DECEMBER

TUESDAY—DECEMBER 1.

A MINISTER friend of ours has in his study a copy of Albrecht Dürer's famous picture, "Praying Hands", which shows two hands together in the attitude of prayer.

My friend says that when his small daughter first noticed this picture she exclaimed, "Oh, look, Daddy! A man clapping his hands!"

"I smiled at the time," he told me, "but since then I've thought, 'there's some truth in what she said. For when we pray, don't we put our hands together in joy?' "

I look at that famous picture now and see it in a new light, thanks to that little girl.

WEDNESDAY—DECEMBER 2.

WE spend a lot of time talking about the weather — it is supposed to be one of our chief topics of conversation — and a lot of our time we grumble about it!

It was with this in mind that the Lady of the House and I invented a little game we play from time to time. Whoever is first up and looks out of the bedroom window has to make a comment about the weather — but it has to be a cheerful one, whatever the conditions.

Sometimes, of course, it's easy — "A lovely sunny morning!" But rain? "Nice refreshing rain this morning, Francis!" And a stormy wind? "This will blow the cobwebs away!" Even fog? "Well, I think grey is a lovely colour!"

Try it — it will test your ingenuity, and cheer you up no end!

THE FRIENDSHIP BOOK

YOU'VE heard the old saying, "As one door shuts, another opens" and I hope you have found it to be true. Miriam Eker has, and she has written a poem about it:

> *One door shuts — another opens,*
> *   That's what people say,*
> *A very clever proverb,*
> *   For it often works that way.*
>
> *A sudden change of fortune,*
> *   A sudden slender purse,*
> *And we think that Fate is cruel,*
> *   That it couldn't be much worse.*
>
> *But when we feel our patience*
> *   Is very sorely tried,*
> *Quite suddenly a door appears,*
> *   That's open very wide.*
>
> *When doors are shut before us,*
> *   We're bound to feel depressed,*
> *But when another opens wide,*
> *   We find it's for the best!*

IN William Canton's "Invisible Playmate" he tells the beautiful story of a father who wanted to give his little girl one great imperishable memory. He took her out in the dark one clear night so that she would always remember the star-studded sky, and her father holding her by the hand. Beauty, stillness, security, love — they would all be mingled in her memory.

Fortunate the child to have such a father.

THE FRIENDSHIP BOOK

I DON'T think the Lady of the House and I ever come away from visiting our old friend Mary without receiving some bit of wisdom which makes us feel that she does us more good on our visits than we can possibly do her.

The other day our conversation turned, for some reason, to the subject of sleep.

" Sleep?" said Mary, " I sleep like a top. You know my secret?"

" No," we replied.

" Well," said Mary, " I've got a comfortable bed and a comfortable mind. They're better than any sleeping pills!"

I WILL lay me down in peace, and take my rest: for it is thou, Lord, only, that makest me dwell in safety.   Psalm 4, 8

JOSEPH ROWNTREE was a prosperous chocolate and cocoa manufacturer and a generous philanthropist. There came a time when he decided that he and his family were far too wealthy so, with their agreement, he gave away half his fortune to the poor.

He was a Quaker, a man of simple habits and great integrity. His grandson has told how, on one occasion, his grandfather found himself travelling in a first class rail compartment. This was against his principles as he always travelled second class. So, to get right with his conscience, the next time he had to make a train journey he bought a first class ticket and travelled second class.

THE FRIENDSHIP BOOK

TUESDAY—DECEMBER 8.

EVERYBODY likes a person who looks on the bright side. Here is a short verse that sums it up:

What one approves, another scorns,
And thus his nature each discloses;
Some find the rosebush full of thorns,
Some find the thornbush full of roses.

WEDNESDAY—DECEMBER 9.

THERE are many who have had a street or building named after them because of some outstanding contribution they have made to the life of a community, but there must be few who have had a town called after them. There is, however, in the North-east of England, the new town of Peterlee, which was named after a well-known local man.

Peter Lee was a Durham miner who, till he was 30, lived a rather wild, disreputable and vagrant life not only in this country, but in America and Africa, too. Then he became a Christian, joining Wheatley Hill Methodist chapel where he was an active local preacher and Sunday School teacher. Then he took up public life on the local council and later the county council on which he served as Chairman for many years.

He was greatly respected for his Christian character and selfless service, and it seemed completely right that the new town should be named after him.

Few of us are likely to receive that sort of honour, but we can be remembered for service and friendship, helpfulness and self-sacrifice. We could have no better memorial.

THE FRIENDSHIP BOOK

IN Great Yarmouth, applicants for pensioners' bus passes were asked to produce a passport-type photograph. One woman in her sixties fished out a picture of an attractive young brunette.

When the clerk looked puzzled, she replied, "Oh, yes, it's me. It was taken in 1947."

IN one of his books, the well-known Methodist preacher, the late Dr W.E. Sangster, tells how when he lived in the beautiful old town of Conway in North Wales, he was once expecting a visitor from London. He was glad to see, when the day dawned, that it was bright and sunny. His visitor was to travel by train and Dr Sangster thought of the journey he would be making.

Sangster describes the route from Crewe. . . "the Cheshire Plain with beauty and sunshine, then, after Chester with its walls and great cathedral, the train is roaring down the North Wales coast. The Sands of Dee stretch away to the right, and across the estuary the sun plays on Hoylake and West Kirby; the Welsh hills begin to rise on the west; there is a glimpse of the marble Church at Bodelwyddan, Rhyl, Abergele, the glorious sweep of Colwyn Bay; a peep of the Little Orme — then Conway, gateway to Snowdonia."

He then tells how, when his visitor arrived, he jumped out of the train, exclaiming, "I'm glad that's over. It was so grimy in the Potteries!"

No doubt it had been. But all the rest of the journey had been sheer beauty!

Perhaps we're all a little like that man at one time or another—making much of the discomforts and pains of life and taking the joys for granted.

PROUD MAJESTY

THE FRIENDSHIP BOOK

WHEN the Scottish poet Edward Borland Ramsay was getting on in years he wrote these moving lines in which he expressed his simple faith:

> *I hold Life's taper in my hand,*
> *And watch it slowly burn away;*
> *And well I try to understand*
> *The meaning of each passing day,*
> *And often to myself I say:*
> *"There is a lasting light to come,*
> *That will not flicker, fade away,*
> *To leave my soul in endless gloom."*
> *I hold aloft my feeble light —*
> *God take and make it ever bright.*

STAND in awe, and sin not: commune with your own heart, and in your chamber, and be still.

Psalm 4, 4

YEARS ago, in the days of great open hearths, the burning of the Yule Log was a common feature of Christmas festivities. The log, often decorated with greenery and ribbons, was carried ceremoniously into the house and kindled with a piece of last year's log kept specially for the purpose. In the same way, a piece of the new log was kept for next year's ceremony.

It reminds me of something a friend of ours is fond of saying: "The trouble is that we talk of 'keeping Christmas', but we don't keep it. We let it go!"

This year, let us resolve to keep alive the spirit of Christmas, just as they used to keep a fragment of the Yule Log.

THE FRIENDSHIP BOOK

I LIKE the advice given by an older man to a young colleague who had become depressed by the failure of a project on which he had set his heart, and who didn't seem to have the spirit to pull himself together and try again.

"Remember," said the old man, "if one swallow doesn't make a summer, neither does one failure make a perpetual winter." Wisdom there — and encouragement!

WEDNESDAY—DECEMBER 16.

WHEN we were out walking recently, the Lady of the House suddenly stopped and exclaimed, "Francis! My bracelet!" She had just realised that it was no longer on her wrist.

She thought for a moment and then said, "You know, Francis, when we climbed over the stile near the farm, I remember knocking my hand on the top of the post. I wonder if the bracelet fell off then?" Back across the fields we went, and sure enough, there it was at the foot of the stile. It pays to go back sometimes.

Everybody knows of John Bunyan's book, "The Pilgrim's Progress", but I wonder how many are familiar with C. S. Lewis's allegory "Pilgrim's Regress" in which he imagines the pilgrim coming back over the ground again and seeing things afresh in the light that had been given to him at the end of his first journey.

We put great emphasis on "progress", on looking forward and going forward. These are important, but there is also a time for going back — remembering our blessings, and learning from our mistakes. The end of the year is ideal for doing that — and we may discover "lost treasure" as the Lady of the House and I did.

THE FRIENDSHIP BOOK

RECENTLY I came across an article describing the ways in which children in different countries prepare for Christmas — hanging up their stockings in this country, putting out their wooden sabots in The Netherlands, and so on.

One way of giving smaller gifts, which I had not heard of, comes from Germany. They are wrapped in a ball of wool which a girl then uses for knitting. As the wool unrolls, the gifts drop out one by one — perhaps a sweet, a ring, a brooch or other small trinkets. The largest and best gift is right in the centre of the ball.

I couldn't help thinking that every year is a little like that, for each season has its special gifts — the celebrations of New Year, the flowers of Springtime, the delights of Summer holidays, the gorgeous colours and the fruits of harvest-time; even Winter with its long nights with a book before the fire. Then, to crown it all, the joy of Christmas. No wonder somebody, in a prayer, has thanked God for "the varied gifts of use and loveliness which every season brings".

THE church discussion group was talking about prayer and particularly the problem of what seems sometimes to be unanswered prayer. Sitting quietly for most of the meeting was an old lady who had known much trouble in her life, but whose faith had never faltered.

Suddenly she said, "I don't think God always answers prayer . . . " She paused and it was obvious that she was going to say something else. Quietly, she added, "But He always answers the pray-er."

TRUST

When you face the challenge of distant hills
Both real and in the mind,
Allow the hand which made them both
To guide your steps — you'll find
Courage when weary, ready to drop;
Support and strength to reach the top.

THE FRIENDSHIP BOOK

LIZZIE LOVELL was a worker in a boot factory. I know nothing else about her, except that she wrote these two encouraging verses:

> Blest be the sacred tie that binds,
> In friendship's golden tether,
> In every nation, every clime,
> The hearts of men together.
>
> Blest be the pure, unselfish love
> That seeks to help another,
> The love that owns in every man,
> Howe'er debased, a brother.

BEHOLD, a virgin shall be with child, and shall bring forth a son; and they shall call his name Emmanuel, which being interpreted is, God with us.   Matthew 1, 23

IT seems a long time ago now that large houses were staffed by great retinues of servants. Whether a family could keep its servants or not depended, very largely, upon the way in which they were treated.

This is well-illustrated by the following delightful reminiscence of someone who remembers those days. It was Christmas time and the staff all received gifts from the mistress of the house. The cook took hers, thanked her mistress and then said, "I'm sorry I haven't got enough money to buy *you* a present. Instead, I will try to serve you better next year."

Could we give anyone a better present than by resolving in any and every way "to do and be better" next year?

THE FRIENDSHIP BOOK

I READ recently of a portrait photographer who said that he could only take a really good photograph if he could persuade his sitters to smile not simply with their mouths, but with the eyes, too. A "mouth smile", he said, tended to be stiff and artificial, but when he said something pleasant, which brought a smile to their eyes, then the rest of the face took care of itself.

Good advice, not only for when we are having a photograph taken, but for everyday life, too. If we can learn to look and listen for the things which can give us "smiling eyes", we will be able to spread a good deal of happiness and find some for ourselves.

THERE is an old legend that, on their way to Bethlehem, the Three Wise Men quarrelled about which of them was taking the most precious gift to the Christ Child — the gold, the frankincense or the myrrh.

Then, as they looked up at the sky, the star they had been following suddenly disappeared from sight. They continued as best they could until they came to the edge of a village where a group of people was gathered round a shallow well that had dried up.

The Wise Men were carrying bottles of water for their journey and each of them poured a little into the well so that the thirsty villagers might share it. As the three bent over the well they saw a star reflected in the water, and looking up saw that their guiding light had returned.

It's only legend, yet how true it is that the real meaning of Christmas is in giving and sharing and caring.

THE FRIENDSHIP BOOK

MOST people know and love the carol "Silent Night" but I wonder how many realise that in the little Austrian village of Oberndorf where it was written in 1818, there is a Silent Night Society?

Each Christmas Eve, the Mayor of Oberndorf leads a silent procession of children through the streets to the church. Members of the Silent Night Society ring the bells, then there is another period of silence before the singing of the now-famous carol. Wreaths are laid on the graves of Franz Gruber and Josef Mohr — the schoolmaster/organist and the village priest who wrote the carol.

I like, on Christmas Eve, to keep a moment of silence, to hum the words quietly to myself, or listen to the tune sung. I think, in that way, the Silent Night Society is larger than the little group in Oberndorf, that it stretches across the world, composed of all those who love the carol and share its sentiments of hope and peace.

PHYLLIS BIRCHALL wrote these moving lines:

Faith is like a shining star, beckoning us from afar,
Faith means trusting, come what may,
Even when the day seems grey,
Looking upward to the sun, knowing God loves
everyone.
When courage fails, but faith remains, this will lift
us up again,
But if faith begins to dim, let your thoughts just
dwell on him,
Who for us came down to earth, to save and bless us
with His birth.